RELIGIOUS
EQUALITY
REFUTED

I0460861

BY GREGORY HEARY

Do all religions lead to heaven? Imagine you are going to the store in order to purchase something perfect to drink. Immediately after entering you see a brand name drink close to the cash register, do you buy it because it's the first one you were exposed to, or because it's the one your parents buy and drink that they fed you all your life? If you go past the first display you come across another, but the 2nd brand is expired, do you give up and say there must not be any drink for me because all I've experienced so far in the store wasn't any good? If you continue looking you discover there is a big 99% sale on a colorful drink, do you buy it just because it's the cheapest in the store requiring the least from you to obtain your goal? If you continue another brand is discovered, but it's not very popular and you've never heard of it before, do you just buy it so you can get out of the store? If you go on eventually you pass the displays and reach the drink section, on the lowest shelf there is an energy booster drink that gives adrenaline upon consumption, do you buy it and suffer the withdrawals after the sugar high is gone, or do you get trapped paying more and more for less and less of a fix? There is a coupon for another drink that comes with a free gift, but are you going to buy a drink just because of the perks it comes with? If you go on you see the popular sweet drinks loaded with artificial flavor, they're easy to swallow, everyone knows and loves the brand even if they don't buy it, but you know it has no nutritional value and the ingredients aren't even listed. Then nearly running out of patience you examine a health drink, sure it's healthy but you can't even imagine how anyone could drink such a thing once, let alone daily. Then the store employee recommends a drink to you and suggests it's the best there is they've tried them all, coincidentally it's also the most expensive which you would have to charge in order to buy since it's beyond your means to afford. Amazingly the store employee leaves you alone and makes the sales pitch to another who buys it. You give up, you've seen all there is, every drink has some type of problem and none of them are perfect, might as well leave and never drink anything.

Suddenly you get a glimpse of something, it's almost as though it's been hidden from you since you walked into the store. This drink is on the top shelf, so it takes a lot of effort to climb to reach it, from this high level you see everything below differently than how it appeared to you when you were on the ground. This drink is not a popular brand among your friends or family, you've heard of it before but never paid it any serious attention or consideration. This time you examine it closely, the ingredients are even healthier than those in the health drink, except it actually tastes good; although it's an acquired taste that takes time to get used to. While it's not the cheapest, it's not the most expensive either, it costs you more than others but it is something you can realistically afford. Eventually after serious contemplation you decide to bring it home and start drinking it every day for every meal. Some of your friends and family ridicule your decision and tell you to buy what they're buying, or to try something else. But you've done your research, in your heart and mind you know that it is the right drink and nothing else will bring satisfaction after you've tasted the best, in fact because they're human it's the right drink for them as well however they don't care to try it, even if they let you tell them about it. It's sad really, because you know what they're drinking and realize its inferiority, you yourself used to drink it. You are aware of how when you were drinking the junk you also thought there was nothing better, until you searched for perfection and found it.

This search for the perfect drink is an analogy to the search for the true religion. It's not easy, it might require a sacrifice of time, energy, money, and serious thought, but the best things in life all do, so why would the most important thing in life be any different? Sure you could make your decision based solely on whether it's the cheapest, the easiest, the sweetest, the healthiest, the most popular, the first one you had or because some "expert" recommended it, however if you did that in any other aspect of life outside of religion under no circumstances would it be considered an intelligent decision. Ask yourself why do you have the religion you do? Did you even make the decision? Was it made in haste, without examining all the available options? What are the consequences of making the wrong decision? If we take all this into account when choosing a drink, then we should give the same courtesy to religion.

Pagans were religiously inclusivistic and didn't think beliefs were significant or relative to personal religions. There was no such concept as heresy in ancient pagan religions. Pagans had a different god to pray to for every specific need, similar to how today there is a "saint" to pray to for every specific need. Pagans believed that you didn't necessarily have to worship a certain god or follow the teachings of a certain temple, as long as you prayed to some gods then you were ok, it didn't matter which gods you prayed to or how, it was only important that a person have belief in some of the gods and did some type of worship. Pagans believed that only atheists were wrong and as long as you believed in a religion you were right and would be rewarded in the afterlife. According to the pagans the "gods" would only punish someone who didn't believe in any of the various religions. They viewed the afterlife as if it were a card game, thinking as long as someone played some cards then they'd be guaranteed to win big, because they all felt special. Polytheism was a major theological gambling industry.

Many people think that it doesn't matter what you believe, thinking all good people of all religions go to heaven and only evil people go to hell, all you have to do is believe in God, it doesn't matter what religion you are. If that's the case we should also say: *"It doesn't matter what school you go to, it doesn't matter what country you live in, it doesn't matter what job you have and it doesn't matter who you marry."* Choosing which religion you practice is more important than all of these other decisions combined and your religion will affect all your other decisions. This doctrine of multiple religions being valid is called Monolatrism. Monolatrism is the belief in and worship of one God without at the same time denying that others can with equal truth worship different gods. Many people think this is just religious tolerance, but it is actually a religion in itself called Monolatrism. Sadly many people are Monolatrists and don't know it. There is one big reason why it does matter what religion someone practices, it matters because we have an enemy who wants us to disobey our Creator and get punished for it eternally. Keeping this in mind it is easy to see how this statement that "it doesn't matter which religion you are" is truly one of the most satanic statements that exist, Satan himself would be hard pressed to come up with a more evil statement. Realistically if you met Satan face to face and he could only say one thing to you in order to lead you astray, it would probably be: "*it doesn't matter what religion you are, as long as you believe in God you'll go to heaven*". Another prevalent statement is "*let's agree to disagree*", which originated from the pagan Greek philosophers. Realistically mature adults can just disagree, it is illogical to think a disagreement can only take place if it is mutually agreed to. None of the prophets would ever make such a statement and we shouldn't use the mottos of pagans in our conversations today, by agreeing to disagree it means that the matter involved is trifling. Oftentimes this statement places more value on people's feelings than on what is right and wrong. If you disagree with me then we disagree, it doesn't mean we turn to violence automatically becoming bitter enemies because we don't "agree to disagree". To agree to disagree means to say the matter is something where it's perfectly fine to be completely wrong. When it comes to religion people are able to disagree because of freewill, but that doesn't mean it's ok and not a crime in the sight of God to disagree with certain doctrines. If one doctrine is true and right nobody should disagree with it, some will but to agree to disagree means you thinks it's good for someone to disagree with the truth. No wise person goes into a conversation planning that no matter what after all is said and done then all sides will disagree. If that is the case then what is the point of having a discussion? Why even bother talking to such bigots? Pagan Greek philosophers would "agree to disagree" before they even argued because they thought practically every religious opinion was ok to have or valid and just liked to bicker. They agreed to disagree so each knew that no matter what was said they would both leave with conflicting opinions regardless of which was right because they just wanted to have fun arguing, even if they didn't personally believe the idea they were arguing on behalf of, and even if they did end up agreeing they would purposely disagree with each other because they had previously agreed to disagree prior to the debate. Also it was considered dishonorable and shameful to change one's opinion, even if one knew it was wrong. This may also be a reason why the pagans had multiple deities, because otherwise they'd have to admit some things are undeniably true and cannot be disagreed with, which would have endangered their entire entertainment industry. To idolaters more gods meant more jobs. Philosophy was basically Greek entertainment where they sat around having passionate ideological arguments for the thrill of arguing in order to feel/appear intellectually superior by outwitting or arguing better than their opponent(s). Greek philosophy was pagans debating for fun/fame. It's impossible to argue that one cannot argue, likewise it's impossible to agree to disagree, because then you would be in agreement. Which is why this pagan statement is the epitome of stupidity, merely being the slogan of pacifism, arrogance, ignorance and the catchphrase for socially acceptable uncondemned bigotry. To be indifferent to religions and religious opinions is a religious belief in itself, and it's not the religion taught by any prophet. God has never ever told mankind, "*You should all just get along, I love everybody. However and whoever you worship and whatever you believe about me it's all the same to me.*" That's psychotic,

6

not prophetic. If you believe every religion counts then you are upon a falsehood that God hates and punishes.

Throughout time these popular pagan doctrines of *"only atheists go to hell"* and *"agreeing to disagree"* in order to avoid sore feelings has led to the formulation of what I refer to as the 21st century paganism. Which is the theory that, *"I'll just live life as I see fit while being good to everyone, I don't need a religion or rules to tell me how to treat people or what to do in life. As long as I don't displease anybody then why would I get punished by God? That is, if there even is a God or afterlife."* This is a combination doctrine of American freedom and democracy, which causes people to think they are entitled to a pursuit of happiness and that the majority opinion is correct, along with the Santa Claus methodology and a touch of polytheistic gambling. First of all you will never please everybody, so the theory fails right there. Secondly how do you know what is good treatment to someone? An oppressed spouse or abused child will think their family is alright and normal if they never learn that domestic abuse is wrong and abnormal. If you get served unhealthy toxic edibles all your life, you'd consider that "good cooking" even though in reality it's poisoning you. This even applies to "fresh air", urban and rural peoples have a very different definition of "good fresh air" and if the rural person smelled what the urban city dweller considered "good fresh air" they'd laugh and cite how the pollution is toxically nauseating. Yet cityfolk believe and say the air they breath is good/fresh. Thus "good" is a matter of debate of which there are many different and contradictory definitions. So the idea that someone will know how to treat others good is flawed because an individual human doesn't even know what's good for their own health without being told, let alone knowing what the proper way to treat everyone else is in every situation in life. Basically these people use their own definition of "good treatment" or the opinion of their modern culture thinking the popular opinion is best, when usually the masses are the most unjust and oppressive type of group there is. Those people who think they'll just treat others how they want to be treated and that is what "good treatment" is are also unjust because people don't know how they are supposed to treat themselves and they frequently degrade and ridicule themselves as a result of low self-esteem and Satanic whispers. Also they forget that if a person is insane or stupid then if they followed this idea of treating others as they want to be treated, havoc and chaos would destroy us all, but of course those who believe in this idea never suspect they could possibly be stupid or insane. Really they never ever consider that they could be too stupid to know how to treat someone else justly, they just assume since they are human then they know how to treat other people correctly. Yet nearly everyone on the planet thinks the same thing, so unless there are no stupid people on earth then it's impossible for people to treat people correctly without instructions. Whereas "instructions on how to treat others" is one of the traits of religion. So the person who claims "I can treat other people good without religion." is simply a fool who has a religion without even knowing it. And if you don't know what your religion is then it's probably satanic in some way and stupid/wrong. While even intelligent people have different expectations of what is good treatment and what is bad treatment, so even the genius would end up mistreating people without knowing it. Typically this philosophy/faith stems from trust issues where a person has had a bad experience with other humans or authority and would have preferred to have been treated differently than they were, so Satan leads them to think that their idea of treating others is the apex of morality. In short they incorrectly think they know what "good treatment" is. They religiously believe this because if they admit that they don't know what good treatment is then they might possibly be a "bad person" and those who they deeply feel were bad to them might not actually be as bad or evil as they feel/think them to be. Yet nobody likes to imagine they are self-victimizing extremists, we always feel we have the "right amount of resentment" and never resent those who wrong us more than they deserve. Although in reality these types tend to always be extra sensitive to how others treat them, particularly if they don't get the "good treatment" they give to others in return. Fundamentally their doctrine stems from them thinking they are a good person based on their interactions, ideas or experience. It can be tricky to teach them they don't know what is good or bad without divine instruction because they interpret that to mean they are an evil person and they don't "feel evil". In summary they are theologically stupid but feel smart. However the bigger issue with this false notion is that religion is primarily about how you treat others. This is a false notion. Religion is about your relationship with your Creator. How you treat others is just one part of religion, which is only a part of religion because the Creator makes rules for how you are to interact with his other creatures similar to how a boss has a company policy for how to treat other employees. At the end of your shift your job is about doing what your boss put you in the work environment to do, your treatment of co-workers is only a minor aspect of your job, it's not the purpose of your existence nor should it be your main focus. At the end of the day if you treat all your coworkers good that doesn't make you a good employee nor entitle you to a day's worth of pay. There is much more to the test of life than getting along with others and you can't figure out how to properly treat coworkers unless the boss of the Universe tells you how. Any employee who claims to be a good employee because they treat other employees good without even reading the manual for co-worker conduct and rejects the fact they have to follow what it says to be a good employee is a lying fool about to get fired for insubordination regardless of how they treat others. These same caring people who care so much about being good to others seem to have no qualms with rejecting the prophethood and authority of prophets. Honestly they don't give a damn what a prophet says they have to believe or do. So in reality they are selective about how they are "good to others" and are contradictory in their doctrine. They are caught between wanting complete independence of people such as prophets, yet at the same time want to be nice to everyone and live in harmony. This is their contradiction, because they can't treat prophets good if they disobey or disbelieve in them. So they oppress and abuse prophets in the name of treating people good without believing in religious regulations. Their root problem is that they are afraid of authority figures dictating their lifestyle because they have suffered oppression in the past and have been deluded by the gospel of freedom which says all rules are oppressive, despite them turning the "golden rule" that was preached by Confucius into their only rule. That's what's so funny about their "I don't have rules except for treating people nicely" dogma is that this is itself a traditional religion preached by other people who also said people need to believe and do certain things which the religious authority says to believe and do. Confucius though taught more than just the "golden rule", he basically taught people, *"Do what our government says and be good to your family and countrymen."* This is a childish belief. Confucius was a confused intellectual/spiritual child. The mythical "good kid" as advertised by pop culture believes in diluted Confucianism. The "bad children" have a very similar belief, except it circumvents the family worship taught by Confucius. These types don't want to follow the rules their parents give them for their own safety and they don't understand why their parents get upset and/or punish them for breaking a rule in which they aren't hurting anyone else; not realizing the rule they broke was designed to prevent them from hurting themselves. In adult version such children become anarchistic not seeing how religious rules aren't meant to be oppressive but are meant to prevent humans from breaking themselves in self-oppression. The religion of anarchy basically teaches that as long as it's consensual by adults then it's legal/okay and shouldn't be banned/forbidden. Mutual or individual adult consent is the deity of anarchy and coercion/censorship/inequality/judgment are the anarchist's definition of sins/crimes. This childish belief has led to movements for the legalization of drugs, illicit sex, crimes and all other kinds of individually destructive habits because people forget that oppressing yourself is just as bad as oppressing others. In reality oppression is forbidden for everyone even if one chooses to oppress oneself. To let someone oppress themself can be a sin. Thus Muhammad pbuh taught in authentic hadiths "*Help your brother regardless of whether he is wrongdoer or a person who is wronged.*" He was asked how could one help their brother(in faith) if he was a wrongdoer when Islam forbids wrongdoing? Muhammad pbuh explained, "*Restrain and prevent him from wrongdoing, for that, indeed, is helping him.*" Religiously you do not have the right to pursue happiness if that happiness involves oppressing yourself or harming yourself, Satan says you do but God says you don't. Some religiously anarchistic believe self-oppression is bad but then what happens when self-interest conflicts with treating others good? Are they going to "help someone" by restraining and preventing them from doing wrong? Or will they think that's not "good treatment" since it may well upset the person being prevented from evil. On the one hand self-interest or self-preservation takes precedent in some scenarios but in others self-sacrifice is better. Yet how does one determine when self-interest or self-sacrifice is the better course of action? In such situations it is impossible to trust yourself because you will be biased to side with self-interest and thus eventually end up treating others unjustly and badly despite the whole claim behind rejecting religion being that "I treat others good so I'm a good person." Such people are posers because when the going gets tuff and they have to bleed in order treat others good they usually won't and if they do sometimes they will do so when they shouldn't because of their fanaticism in treating others good. What's worse is these people will sometimes cite Jesus pbuh as an example of how people should treat everyone how they want to be treated and "turning the other cheek" etc and in this saying they imply that they are living religion even though they reject it and

11

that those who follow the rules and believe in doctrines are like the hypocritical Pharisees. But did the Pharisees think Jesus pbuh treated them good or "as they wanted to be treated"? No, the "golden rule" did not apply to everyone because that guideline alone cannot be taken out of context nor can it replace religion in totality. Yet the non-religious claim religious folk are like the Pharisees but in reality Jesus pbuh was more like the Pharisees than he was these people who say they don't believe in religion but just believe in treating everyone good as some of them falsely claim was what Jesus pbuh really meant and taught people. To avoid becoming a slave of a religion they become a slave of people who never give them clear rules for slavehood and are never satisfied with their performance anyways. Therefore the religion of those who think they can "just be good" and God will reward them when they die is entirely a religious placebo and byproduct of humanistic tribalism. While they may do many good deeds, religiously they are crazy on the lowest of theological and intellectual levels. Sadly though others are so pleased with their manners they enable such people in believing they are good despite being traditionally faithless. What's worse is that when some of these "faithless good-doers" die, frequently those who know them will feel confident they are going to paradise because they "treated people good" as religions say we should do despite them not believing in a religion. Personally I hate when this happens because hellfire is their abode despite all their "good treatment" of others because God requires belief in a religion to go to paradise. Yes you get points on the test of life for "good behavior" but you can't get to paradise on good deeds alone. The "good people" don't go to paradise, you have to be a believer as well. A bad believer can go to paradise but a "great disbeliever" is doomed for hell, because God makes the rules and has ruled belief in the right religion is that important that it trumps "good behavior". This doesn't mean believers can be bad, no they should be better than all disbelievers but in theory belief in the true religion is a better deed than the best deed towards others which a

12

disbeliever can do. Hence in reality the disbeliever is always an "evil good-doer" and while a believer can be a "good evil-doer". So theologically in full context there is no "good disbeliever" or "bad believer" because belief weighs heavy on the scales. From our standards we could have "good disbelievers" or "bad believers" but our standards of goodness in people differs from the standards of the Creator of everything. Yet if there were any real good in a person then God would guide them to the true religion hence in a real sense there is no "good disbeliever". Which is why it's so aggravating when these "faithless good-doers" die and some idiots claim they are going to paradise because they were "good people". The faithless can never be "good people", they can possible be "good to people" but being good to people itself is not enough to make one a good person, despite what "faithless good doers" claim. Thus they aren't good people despite people thinking they're good because they are good to people. Also just because they may believe a God exists, does not mean they believe in God and thus qualify for paradise, nearly everybody believes that a God exists on their deathbed. Yet just believing a God exists is not enough for God to love you. God can still, and does, hate many who believe a God exists. Simply believing there is a God, is like having baby level faith, for a baby that's pretty good but for an adult most have no excuse to have such a incomplete understanding about God and the true religion. Those who merely believe a God exists practically have "baby level faith" which is sinful because they aren't a baby so they are below the minimum amount of faith which they are required to have. Sadly though many think that's all you need to believe in order to go to paradise and thus go to hell forever with such a belief. Yet the masses say they are going to paradise after they die! Which is not only wrong but it's extremely sinful to think/claim even if it's just to "be nice" or help console others. Nobody can lie about the destination of the dead especially when it's known what destination awaits them with certainty, and yes with some people who die, and I've met some and am "related" to

13

some, it is known with certainty whether they will burn in hell forever or not. Fundamentally the beliefs of these "faithless good doers" believe actions speak louder than doctrines and that if you worshipped Satan or a statue but treated everyone else good then you would be a good person. It is common for this type of belief to result from bad parenting or arrogance, but many factors contribute to it. Although if it stems from bad parenting then it can poison an entire family tree. It's primarily because people experienced bad relationships with people in the past that they think having good relationships with people is so important. It's because they wish they had good relationships they automatically think everyone values them just as much and they naturally extend this idea to think that their idea of what's good treatment is the correct definition, ultimately leading them to think God values "good treatment" as much as they do and that their definition of God is the same as God's. The intentions of such people are noble and they can be quite friendly and kind individuals, but their belief is satanic and complete filth because it eliminates God and denies his authority over us as well as his wisdom and our obligation to be grateful for all the gifts God has given to us. It is because they don't know God they think he doesn't know them and thus couldn't possibly know what's best for them, so they are scared to trust him to regulate their affairs especially since there are so many scams out there with false prophets and man-made religions that have been made for oppressing people. Tragically these people have been scared away from religion by the hypocrites and organizations who use religion for oppression, manipulation and exploitation. Satan led them to disbelief in the name of goodness free from hypocrisy, theology, confusing rules they find hard to understand and possible scams from religious hierarchies. While the adherents of this false religion are disorganized it's ideology is very popular and many subscribe to it. It starts with the notion of nonconformity being praiseworthy or a type of independence. Yet all of us must conform to something or else we wouldn't have an

14

identity or a range of likes and dislikes. Even if one claims that they are not conforming then they are submitting to the popular ideal myth of not conforming and do indeed conform to that ideal. The main reason people think non-conformity is such a good thing is because they are trained that diversity is some type of sacred institution. While it's true that conformity is counter to diversity it is within all of us whenever we agree. Thus to truly be independent you are obligated to disagree with everyone about everything, otherwise you are conforming to something. As a result they disagree with every religion because they fear conforming to a traditional religious faith. To sum it up this faith is a belief in customized religion, where each person makes their own. Essentially every member of this religion belongs to their own special denomination, which they created individually and only they can follow. Religiously this means they are claiming prophethood for themselves and that everyone is a prophet and knows best how to treat everyone else. It's because this religion is completely crazy that they never try to convert others to it but will only use it to defend their lifestyle/faith. Ironically their issue is with oppressive man-made religions and as a result they were led by Satan to oppress themselves with their own self-made religion. Unfortunately the shackles they put on themselves are harder to get off than the shackles people put on others. The trouble is they fail to understand their anti-religion attitude is actually a religion in itself with them as god; since they treat others how they see fit instead of how the Creator of those people sees fit. Thus they are a blend between an atheist, an agnostic and a polytheist, because some believe in a god while some don't yet in reality they give everyone the authority of God. A quick way to refute this faith is to say people are stupid and aren't qualified to determine what good treatment is even in large numbers, as is evident in that popular opinions of good and bad change faster and more frequently than the weather. Just tell them people are too stupid to know how to be good. God has to teach us how, when and why to be good. The only questions are who is God, what does God want, and how do we learn what God wants from us in every situation in life? Only a religion is capable of answering these questions satisfactorily but lots of faiths give the wrong answers. However fundamentally only a religion qualifies to be right. Nobody can get the right answers without the right religion. To not choose a religion is to be just as wrong as those who choose a religion which is wrong. Choose wisely, but choose. Its impossible not to, everyone is choosing every second they live. The first part in choosing correctly is realizing a choice must be made and that you will be making it before you die, even if you think you aren't or don't want to and try not to. Everyone believes a religion, but the prophets only taught 1.

First we have to define God and what determines whether a person is good and what determines if a person is evil. This is where the religious equality theory falls apart because each religion teaches different things that contradict the teachings of other religions. If none of them can agree on the definition of God then they are even less likely to agree on what is good and what is evil. For example some Jews say Ezra pbuh is the son of God, some Christians say Jesus pbuh is the son of God, Muslims say God cannot have children. So which is it, does God have kids or not, and if so who? If one believes the wrong thing in that regard then they have the wrong concept of God and essentially don't believe in God as he really is. Having a belief about God does not mean you actually believe in God accurately, you could be believing in a fictional version. Naturally the Creator must be different than the creation. Logically the Creator must be an eternal, self-sufficient, infinite being and rationally there can only be 1. If the Creator needed a creator then we would wonder who created the creator's creator and keep going back to their creators, if everything required a creator then nothing would ever be created, there simply must be something self-existing that started everything. Something cannot come from nothing, something must exist by itself to start with. Since so many things exist that means that something must have always existed. That something is the Creator of everything. Since there can only be 1 Creator then it follows that there can only be 1 religion the divine entity has proscribed for the 1 species of human kind and there is only 1 way to practice it. According to the understanding of the prophets who were all on 1 team, teaching about 1 God, all of them agreed there is only 1 true religion and 1 way to get to paradise. As we search for the true religion let's examine some of the various religious views, hopefully recognizing those which are false, narrowing down the competition to a smaller number so that the selection isn't overwhelming.

Hinduism, Sikhism and Jainism teach reincarnation and that every stone, plant and animal is actually a trapped human being in a different form because of karma. Clearly that is not the case and we would have known and remembered all our previous lives if that were the case. The populations of animals, plants and humans have been rising as well, so where are all these new souls coming from if they are just being recycled? Are they splitting off and dividing into more every time something dies? According to reincarnation a person could die, come back as another person and end up marrying their former mother, sister or daughter. By eating an animal, or even a plant, you could actually be literally eating your dead relative, if reincarnation were true. This idea of a dead person's soul transmigrating to other life forms is known as metempsychosis. A person with this belief is simply afraid of being judged by God and would rather be turned into an animal than face the possible consequences of hell. This stems from the disease of loving this world so much that they cannot bear the idea of life in the grave, or the Day of Resurrection, they hope that they can enjoy this world forever and wishfully think they are reincarnated. This is an example of how sometimes animals are smarter than humans, because animals know they will not be reincarnated and turn into a human if they're a good animal. If reincarnation/karma were a true doctrine, humans would be the most moral of creatures since we would have had an extensive history of "good animal behavior" in order to have reached this state, therefore no human would mess up while they were so close to the top and do the wicked things humans do today if it were true. Also the soul would know what good it did to get to where it is and what bad it did to get to where it is, otherwise no lesson is learned. Reincarnation advocates never state which existed first between animals or humans, because according to the doctrine of reincarnation animals have to exist before humans in order to become them and humans also have to exist before animals in order to become them. Thus the first generation before reincarnation is a paradoxical conundrum. No prophet ever taught that people were reincarnated after death. The idea of reincarnation is evidence of how a man-made religious doctrine has manipulated people and brainwashed them to put up with injustice, racism, abuse and oppression. This idea is inserted into many children's minds through fairytales. Most stories that are believed to develop a child's imagination tend to teach them erroneous religion under the disguise of fantasy. Most of the popular children's *"make-believe"* stories are designed to *"make-them-believe"* in false religious concepts. Whereas many adults get false religious ideas from movies and music which is designed to implant corrupted belief systems, morals, goals and attitudes.

Once while talking to Jehovah's Witnesses, one told me there was no such thing as hell. He basically thought that people who believed in his version of Pauline Christianity, which denies the trinity, will be resurrected to live on earth forever while everyone else will just stay dead. If all the bad people stay dead in a state of nothingness, as they believe, then it would mean justice would never be done. Life would boil down to taking the easy way out of suicide into eternal nothingness, which is what suicides want, or waiting for eternal earthly pleasure. Yet they still believe in Satan, in a nutshell they think he just wants us to miss out on the fun we could have. It'd be nice if Satan were that friendly, but unfortunately he is a hate-filled enemy that desires much worse for us than nothingness. If there is no such thing as hell then why are they so zealous in going door to door? They say because the bible says to, yet in numerous places the bible mentions hellfire even from the mouth of Jesus pbuh. Even the Jews believe in hell, albeit they think that bad Jews will only stay there for 12 months maximum. The first time a Jehovah's Witness told me there was no such thing as hell it left me speechless because I had never met a Christian who didn't believe in hell before. He was trying to convince me Jesus pbuh was the son of God and died for my sins in order to save me from nothingness. He taught God loved me so much he sacrificed his son Jesus pbuh (whom he said created everything and that God only created Jesus pbuh, despite this also being contrary to Genesis and much of the rest of the bible) so that I could be spared the fate of nothingness if I believed it. You can understand why I was speechless, because I was nothing once before, I've already experienced non-existence so it doesn't seem like a "son of God"(whom he said was not divine) would sacrifice themselves to save me from a fate God already put me through. If God didn't want us to experience nothingness, then why did we already experience it? On a separate occasion I spoke to that same man's wife when she came to visit me, she was checking to see where the other Jehovah witnesses were and why they were stuck talking to me instead of walking the streets. This Jehovah's Witness said they do believe in hell. So I heard two different religious opinions from Jehovah Witness husband and wife, the wife believes in hell and the husband doesn't, maybe it's a gender specific belief. This is a problem many people have in that they will preach a religion to others when they don't even know what it teaches, all they know is what "they believe", which more often than not is different than what their religion teaches. Many people just like to preach and seek the comfort of influencing conformity.

May God protect you and me from such a disease. The wife was surprised when I told her that her husband told me in front of her son that there is no such thing as hell. Those Jehovah's Witnesses never came back to chat nor emailed me and I presumed they were trying to sort out amongst themselves what it is they actually believe before they came back, trying to tell me "*the true meaning of the bible*". But 2 other Jehovah's Witnesses came to visit years later and told me that family had moved so they couldn't have come back to visit, then the 2 of them ended up displaying how they believed different things than each other as well. One of them even told me that Jesus pbuh was an angel before he came to earth! (Which contradicts the bible and logic, especially when they also believed that the devil used to be an angel too. Or maybe their version of post angel Jesus pbuh is the same as their post angel devil? What's next will angels become reptiles? Will pigs become birds and fly? Is this some type of reincarnation? Angels are a different species, they can't change into devils or humans or anything else. Once an angel always an angel; without evolution or devolution or pollution.) All three of us were on different theological pages, except they were both using the same book claiming to be of the same religion despite having different beliefs that conflicted with each other. This is why many people think all religions lead to heaven or teach the same thing, because they haven't bothered to research religion in depth. People just hope that they're all the same because if that's the case then they can't be wrong. Since nobody likes to learn they are wrong, they choose not to learn out of the fear of responsibility. The different religions cannot even agree on the existence of heaven and hell, so it is impossible they could all lead to heaven. This is just wishful pacifist thinking because we have been trained by our societies to place more value on the feelings of people than we do on the truth. Thus a religion like Bahaism develops which promulgates this nonsensical notion that all religions are equal. We have become afraid of disagreeing and telling other people they are wrong because people are immature and have poor control over their emotions. It is difficult to disagree politely with mutual respect, but not impossible. Unfortunately one person losing their temper when they're proven wrong can psychologically scar and intimidate a person from ever disagreeing with someone again because they are afraid of being insulted or assaulted, so they avoid potential conflicts at all costs. We must not be afraid to stand up for what is right. However there is a difference between being correct and communicating correctly. It's much harder to communicate correctly than it is to be correct. Although if we learn how and are able to communicate correctly, then when we are correct we must not be afraid of losing popularity or encountering hostile opposition if we are standing up for what is right in the right manner. Although there is a wrong way to communicate the right idea. I ask that you forgive me if I write wrongly and please do not judge the content of what you read to be correct or not based on my writing abilities.

The human mind will not operate without some standard of value, therefore it is impossible for a human not to believe in a god. A god is what creates the standard of value a person has. An example of a standard of value is temperature, the only way to know if you are hot or cold is to have a standard of value, in the case of temperature the standard of value is typically room temperature, but everyone has a different standard of what they consider room temperature to be. One may think they have no religious basis of thought influencing their actions, but they are merely using another name for their god. An atheist bases their argument on faith in indisputable proof, which is their standard of value, or their god. However consciousness itself is an act of faith and no one can actually prove they themselves exist, it requires faith to believe that one exists. Atheists who claim not to believe anything based on faith are actually hypocrites because they have faith that they exist. Your god is the thing you think can control the energy, acts and fate of all individuals; your god is your personal source of morals and creator of the code of conduct by which you will live your life. For some people money qualifies as their god, based on the definition of what a god is, whether they acknowledge money to be their god is irrelevant. What a person worships is what they worship, it doesn't matter if they know what they are worshipping or consider what they are doing to be worship. Worship is a combination between a state of mind and emotions along with a lifestyle and actions that correspond to what their code of conduct is, which they get from their god. If the community you are in determines your sense of right and wrong and behavior, or you believe it controls the energy, acts and fate of all individuals within your community, then the community is your god whether you admit it or not. Many things today hold the position of God unrightfully such as Governments, Media, Wealth, Fame, Knowledge, Democracy, Drugs, Desires, Sex, Science, Technology, Capitalism, Consumerism, Hedonism, Emotions, or "luck"; some people even think the stars are in control of everything and worship the zodiac signs believing in horoscopes. These are all false gods. A false god is something that takes or is given the attributes of God even though they do not fit the description in reality. Paganism is when false gods are made into God based on such incorrect opinions. Unfortunately many pagans will justify these incorrect theories with "evidence" and many people are deceived. Everybody already believes in a god, there is not one person on the planet who doesn't have a form of god. So if believing in a god means you go to heaven then everyone who has ever existed is going to heaven and if that's the case then what and who is hell for? The ancient polytheist pagans would say hell is only for atheists and people collectively seen by the majority or by social customs as evil.

Some people will go to extremes and suggest that heaven is a state of mind. If heaven is a state of mind then is the hellfire a state of mind as well? Such a mindset is insane, dangerous and Satanic. Yet this is what Rastafarians believe, alongside their false notion that Rasta Fari is the black Messiah. When Adam pbuh and Eve were exited from paradise, it wasn't just a mental change that took place. When Enoch pbuh and Jesus pbuh ascended to heaven they didn't go on mental journeys. Satan wants people to think paradise isn't a physical place because he doesn't want humans to go there. By tricking a person into thinking heaven is mental and not physical Satan distracts the person from taking the steps necessary to physically get to heaven. This idea is philosophical and philosophers worship knowledge, but their "knowledge" isn't knowledge, it's oftentimes just complex wit. Most philosophy is just popular idiots propagating false nonsense with short memorable phrases that sound clever, or disguising ignorance with elegant vocabulary. For instance Pythagoras forbid his followers picking up anything that fell off a table, which led Greeks to think whatever food fell on the ground belonged to "the heroes" or ancestral spirits. The Ancient Romans and Prussians also copied this belief while the Germans said such food belonged to the devil. Theses superstitions originate from the philosopher Pythagoras. Aristotle taught that baldness was due to a loss of semen and that boys maimed in the private parts could not grow beards. In 340 BCE in "*The Nicomachean Ethics, V*" Aristotle wrote "*A man may commit adultery with a woman knowing well who she is, but not of free choice, because he is under the influence of passion. In that case he is not an unjust man, though he has done an injustice.*" The stupidity and invalidity of such a philosophy is so well known to women that refutation is unnecessary. However for any women who've ever had a guy cheat on them and been told "It's not my fault." now they know that Aristotle is the guy who gave them this line. These "Great Philosophers" are merely the teachers of the philanderers. While both Aristotle and Pliny taught that the more hair a man had the larger his sexual appetite was and that the sexual appetite of any creature could be extinguished by cutting off their hair. These

23

"great philosophers" taught that getting his hair cut will decrease a man's libido and hair cuts would even work with animals like horses too. Why did they think that? That's philosophy and they were philosophers. Today we have a different word for that called stupidity. Sadly many don't know that stupidity is what you get when you translate the greek word philosophy. This is why wise people consider it an insult to be called a philosopher, whereas foolish people mistake such a label for being a compliment. Just as Satan leads us to think sin will lead to pleasure, these philosophical mentalities are backwards. Philosophy is the abandonment of all authority in favor of individual reason. The "revelation" that philosophy finds nothingness at the end of it's "intellectual" quest leads the philosopher to become a mythmaker through ideology in order to make the world as they see fit. In short philosophers are arrogant idiots who try to think themselves into prophethood. Some even claim to be gods. One such person heavily poisoned by philosphophy frequently tells me their philosophy that "*Heaven is just a state of mind*". Typically just explaining that Adam pbuh and Eve weren't ejected from a state of mind refutes this. However then to avoid being wrong and because they forget my prior refutations, later they repeat their philosophy and claim there is no God and all religions are wrong. So one time I played along and asked this person that, "*If Heaven is a state of mind and all religions are false and there is no God then since you claim to have achieved this heavenly state of mind can you teach me how to get to this state of mind? Or can you teach anyone else here how to experience this heavenly mindset you claim to be enjoying?*" They were speechless. Finally they said no they can't. So I asked them why can't they teach me how to get to this heaven which they say is only a state of mind and I asked why can't I join them in their heavenly mindstate. Again they had no reply so I asked if there was a reason why they could go to this heavenly state of mind and I couldn't and they couldn't teach me. Then they told me that the reason only they can get to this heavenly state of mind is because they are so smart and everyone else, including me, is too

24

stupid. So then I asked how they got so smart and how could I get as smart as them and get to this "heaven" they say is only a state of mind? They said I couldn't because I can never be as smart as them, and then I understood that they are just arrogant and refuse to think anyone else could know more than them about how to live life, so they reject all religions because they can't accept anyone being a prophet because then they would have to admit they are not the smartest person on the planet of all time. Yet as philosophers tend to do, minutes later they "humbly" told me how, *"You know the smarter I get, the more I learn that I don't know anything"*. Whereas this statement is a very true statement indeed, but frequently it is used by arrogant people to make themselves seem humble and open to learning from others. It's similar to how some people claim that they never stop learning, but in reality they've never even started the learning process. It also shows how thoroughly poisoned this individual has been by philosophers, since prior to committing suicide the famous philosopher Socrates said: *"The thing which I know best is that I do not know anything."* (Which then makes it very foolish for people to bother to learn anything of Socrates' teachings when he himself publicly told the world that he does "not know anything" before he died. Thus according to his own words there is literally nothing to learn from him, I guess people just don't know that he publicly said he don't know anything.) Thus later I told this same person who naively thinks that their "Heaven is only a state of mind" philosophy is original, not realizing it's been said by many a fool before them, that the people who take drugs also believe "Heaven is a state of mind" and that's why they "get high" because they believe those drugs will take them to their heaven. They say drugs are the "highway" to the "heaven" of your mind. So the scary thing is that this whole "Heaven is a state of mind" is a very dangerous doctrine because it's the salespitch of every drug dealer. Nearly every drug dealer says this to their clients but then adds the credo that they got the vehicle for you to travel there. However hypocritically this sarcastic stoic also had a framed poster which said "Heaven is above your head and beneath your feet." so they don't even believe their own crap. In reality this philosopher had no coherent religious creed except any and all witticisms that sounded smart to them and spiritually hard for zealous theistic simpletons to refute. Such witty philosophical people make the flaw of thinking that they are so smart and moral they can just use their own reason/judgement to determine what the best way to live is. Nobody else can though because they aren't as smart. This is the fundamental belief of philosophy and philosophers. So what is the whole point of their philosophy and why do they have such catchphrases? It's actually just some stupid thing they think sounds clever to make religious people shutup and stop preaching their religion to them. It's the philosophers way of saying, "*Shutup I don't want to follow any religion because I'm smarter than all these alleged prophets combined and think God doesn't exist and I can learn how to live best by myself because I'm a genius who can tell what's right and wrong all by myself.*" Basically they want to be a "big boy" and don't want a God to tell them what to do or what to think, because they think they're a "big boy" and can figure it all out themselves. They are independent out of fear of ignorant brainwashers without realizing that they are still ignorant independently and can self-stupify while thinking they are discovering the "knowledge of self and the truth about the universe". The problem with this is that reason cannot establish values, believing it can is the dumbest idiotic illusion an imbecile can come up with. The only way someone could ever think that their own idea on right and wrong is correct is if they are arrogant and believe in the Santa Claus methodology. Basically they think they are right because they think they are right and if they were wrong they would know they were wrong or eventually figure it out all by themselves because they believe they are so smart. They think their values are valueable because they value their ability to reason, but who ever said their reasoning abilities were valueable? Well they think and feel it's valueable. So they use their reasoning to prove the value of their reasoning. For example how could "they" possibly be wrong? Them? Of all the people in the world "they" could be wrong?! That's what they consider to be blasphemous heresy when it comes to religion. Their mind doesn't think it could be wrong about important things. With anything else they will quickly and readily admit they can be wrong, but never ever with religion. How could they ever be so wrong about something so important? Because since religion tells people how to live their life and what is right and wrong, they know that if they were wrong about religion then that means they'd be wrong in a major way and would have to make some major intellectual, emotional and lifestyle changes to be right. They don't think it's possible they could be so wrong because of their devout belief in their special "Santa Claus Smarts". Such people think anyone who believes in a religion is stupid and they are smart because they don't. Why do they think that? Because they think they are smart and if they don't believe in any religion they think that means no smart person can, or if one does then they can never be as smart as them because they believe in a religion. Whereas these pseudo-philosophers think religiosity is a ancient mental or emotional disease, or something solely to exploit people or make them feel better. The funny part is they don't know that they actually believe in many religions, so they are actually the dumbest of all religious people because they believe in multiple religious doctrines that are false and they don't even know it. They don't understand what a religion even is but just think religions are institutional organizations built around common core tenets of beliefs, books, principles and rules. Some religions are like that and some aren't but they tend not to know much about religion, only specific reasons why famous and popular ones are false. For instance I've met a white racist who utters this rastafarian "Heaven is a state of mind" line and they don't even know that its a black supremacist rastafarian pot-head religious doctrine. They think they thought of it all by themselves, except they didn't even do drugs to think of it! Thus their super sober intelligence makes stoners look smart, that is if they really are as smart as they feel and say they feel. Ironically the philosophers aren't usually on drugs, because their drug is an overwhelming intoxicating feeling of superior intelligence. Their main problem is that they have spent too much time around very stupid people so they think they are smart because they can tell all the rest of the people they encountered throughout their lives is/was stupid. There are many different degrees of stupidity, they just think because the masses are on a lower level than them then it must mean they are on the highest levels of intelligence. Thereby due to a lack of intellectual company or intellectual superiors they became infected with vanity which turned to insanity. They may claim they are thirsty or hungry for knowledge but by saying such arrogant things they prove their ignorance as to what knowledge even is, because you can't eat or drink knowledge. Or they may say they "love knowledge". If they do then ask them why. Knowledge by itself is useless, unless it is practiced and implemented to serve some good purpose such as pleasing God. They like learning simply because it makes them feel smart and better equipped to argue that they are smarter than everyone else. Although at least these types of people are smart enough to know they can't teach others to be as stupid as they are. Only Satan can teach that type of stupid. I know this is harsh language but philosophers are dumber than dummys. The difference is their complex vocabulary and convoluting linguistic trickery makes them dangerous. They make stupid sound plausible and rational to stupid people. Sorry for using simple words but I don't want to be mistaken for a philosopher. Fools are better people than philosophers. This is because to philosophers life is about vain speculation and sharing quixotic anecdotes, while the fool is smart enough to be silent when corrected and doesn't claim to know anything special or denounce what they don't know. For example one philosopher I know likes to say, *"If God is real then why can't you draw me a picture of God?"* Now my reply to such a person who will think and say religious prohibitions are a cop out, is, "*Have you seen me try to draw? I do not have the artistic abilities required to depict such perfection, <u>nobody does</u>. I can't draw a picture of you either, so does that mean you don't exist? Can you please draw me a picture of your intelligence? I can't.*" Another variation of the "Draw God or else God doesn't exist" ruse is the "*Why doesn't God directly talk to me so I can hear him for myself?*" This can be answered by simply saying that perhaps they are just deaf or can't hear that frequency. Those who are spiritually deaf not being able to hear God doesn't mean God doesn't exist anymore than deaf people at a musical concert claiming they can't hear any music proves that music doesn't exist. Likewise there are insects who live their lives underground and sealife who live thousands of miles underwater and never see/hear humans. What if deep sea creatures said "*Well if these "humans" I've been told about really exist then why have I never seen or heard them? Hey Humans! Show yourselves! That's what I thought, no response. Therefore we must be the dominant most advanced creatures and this place called "land" is a fairytale some idiot told you about. No fish I know has ever been on "land" and came back to tell me about it. So it's not real and deep sea fish are the top of the food chain. The whole world is just water and that's it, don't be so stupid. You have zero proof or a single good reason to believe in land or humans, both are just myths to scare and exploit little gullible fish. Big Smart fish, like me, don't believe in such fantastical gibberish.*" Of course this fictional fish talk doesn't equate to the notion of God because unlike humans God is aware of us and our discussion and cares what we believe. Yet the ideology that lack of visual or audible proof is a proof of nonexistance is adequately proven false by such an example. Ironically these philosophical types tend to have more faith in alien life than they do in God existing. This is because they fear being alone in the Universe. Also if humans were the most advanced species then what is the point of their existance and why would they be the only ones with a planet if life is just created by probability and chance? Probability dictates aliens would exist by chance if humans do, so if they don't then that makes human existance "miraculous" and "unnatural". Hence the popular alien theories began, after WWII and space exploration, to answer the unanswered questions that mass atheism caused and be a proof against certain religions. Aliens have become the new excuse for why people believe in a god. Instead of God being imaginary people have tried to say it was just aliens and the philosophers leeched onto this pathetic atheistic replacement for God, since genuine science confirms a Creator is necessary to explain life on earth, hoping the "aliens" have super-knowledge to help them out of their perpetual circular wheel of philosophical nonsense. Yet if you speak to an average atheist or philosopher about how an alien would go about sending a message to the masses on earth they will agree that it makes perfect sense for an alien to only communicate to those it deemed the best candidates to convey their message to the masses on earth, and that it'd be silly for an alien to try to talk to everyone and visually appear to everyone when they only need to make contact with 1 of us to provide sufficient proof of its existence and tell us what it wanted to tell us. If someone had genuine proof of alien communication and special abilities given to them by the alien, via technology or miracles, most people would accept the human representative of the alien and trust the message they conveyed from the alien to us even though they and the masses never saw or heard the alien themselves. Yet if you replace the word alien with God, the Creator of the Universe, the standards change. Why? This is because with an alien people believe any alien most likely won't want humans to worship it or threaten to punish humans if they don't follow certain rules regarding what they believe and how they live their life. If the alien were to request worship or adherence to alien laws then the humans would rather wage war than be a slave to an alien. Which is actually morally justifiable because the alien didn't create us or our planet so we don't owe the alien anything regarding obedience in our beliefs or deeds. However God did create us and our Universe, so nobody can morally justify going to war with God; plus they know they'd lose if they did. Therefore the only way to morally avoid being a "slave to God" is if God doesn't exist, because if God does exist then it's understood that one has to believe in God's religion and follow God's rules for life or risk the consequences that God alone stipulates. To escape the label of evil being applied to them, the atheist and philosophers pretend God doesn't exist, but because God does exist and is proven to exist they have to play philosophical games regarding what is acceptable proof of God's existence and proof of God's message to humans. These philosophical games are tantamount to practicing a religion wherein the goal is to avoid practicing a religion that has rules which may hinder the fun or freedom that an individual has. Originally philosophy was a religion and it remains one til this day. Philosophy literally translated means "loves Sophia". Sophia was thought to be the incarnate Greek female goddess of wisdom. So philosophy is actually a religion of people who worship arrogant speculative human dumbness, in the feminine form. Philosophers don't know wisdom they just know wise-dumb. Dummys think they're wise and wise ones know they're dumb. Philosophers basically choose to have an imaginary idol of their own imagined intelligence. Most of the ancient pagans knew enough not to worship their own ideas, philosophers don't. They think their thinking will lead them to all types of truth. The less arrogant ones acknowledge human thought is limited so then they give up and say the answers are unknowable because they don't know the answers and if they don't know and can't think of the right answer they think it's impossible for it to be known. Fundamentally philosophers don't believe in genuine prophets of God because they think if God were to choose a prophet then it would've been them. Philosophers tend to be intellectually anti-authoritarian. Philosophy is actually a type of intellectual cult mentality. To the philosopher the only thing they consider sacred is consistent speculation on life/morality/politics/speculation. Philosophy is the religion of arrogant well-spoken speculators. The irony is that despite their view that religions are scams their religion of philosophy is the biggest scam of all time.

When defeated in an argument usually the sour philosopher's emergency liferaft to justify their faith is to boldly put God to the test. They'll say something like *"If God exists then may I be struck down this instant. Since I don't believe in God if God does exist then in order to prove himself he must strike me down right now. Oh I'm still here, I haven't been struck down? I guess God doesn't exist then."* They'll sound very confident when they do this, but it's foolish and this is one of their last excuses to justify disbelief, but it reveals to you that their philosophy teaches hatred for religion and God as well as their stupidity and insincerity. To refute this in America I simply say, *"Ok now, if the U.S. military exists may I be struck down right now with an atomic bomb! Oh wait, that's not fair. Since God is all aware God knows what you said, but IF the U.S. military exists and that's a very big IF then I must pose this challenge where they can hear it. So let's go to a military base and I will say out loud where the U.S. military can hear me "IF the U.S. military exists may I be struck down with an Atomic Bomb right now!" Now since we both know I'm not going to get struck down with an atomic bomb on American soil, this proves the U.S. military doesn't exist because if they existed I would've been immediately bombed upon declaring my challenge. Especially since because of the surveillance and bugging the U.S. does they probably did hear me anyways. That's the same challenge you make to God, so I guess by the same logic the U.S. military does not exist. Unless there is some kind of principle where they don't have to play my game or prove their existence in the way which I demand them to prove their existence. Could it be possible for the U.S. military to exist and not meet my challenge to prove they exist by striking me down with an atomic bomb at the same time?"* If/when the philosopher or atheist says yes, you can reply: *"But if they do exist they have to prove it to me the way I want them to don't they? I mean this is "ME" we are talking about here, they have to listen to ME and play by my rules don't they?"* Then when they say no, you can say, "*Well what if I don't want them to be allowed to prove they exist in any other way? I want to be atomically bombed or else they don't exist. I will not accept any other proof they may show to prove they exist. It's either they strike me down or they don't exist. Do you know why that is? This is because if I'm wrong and the U.S. military were to exist and meet my challenge of Atomically bombing me to prove they exist, I wouldn't know what hit me since I'd be dead. Therefore I can never be proven wrong when saying they don't exist as long as I'm alive.*" The same applies with their game with God. Since if God strikes them down immediately upon demand then what is the point? The person will be destroyed as a disbeliever. God doesn't want that to happen. Thus this philosopher or atheist is basically saying, "*Either I'm right and God doesn't exist, so that means I don't have to practice a religion. Or if God proves he exists by striking me down then I'll be dead so I won't even know I was wrong and still won't have to practice a religion. Therefore I will never ever practice a religion, especially your religion, and can never be proven wrong for not doing so as long as I'm alive. I'm not proving my theory about God not existing to be right or X religion to be wrong, but that's not my goal. I just established a clever excuse to disbelieve. And if you let me play this game with God, you'll never win it. I'm so smart you can't outwit me, and everyone who listens to us talk will think your faith is wrong since I'm totally making you look stupid for believing God exists. Then when you get mad and lose your temper because you can't beat me in a debate, since it's a crooked game, you seem fanatical and I seem right by apparently winning a fair debate by demanding a proof even though I ask for it in a invalid illogical insincere way of demanding proof for God. Stupid fools of our audience will think I'm fair and reasonable never realizing how stupid, insincere or corrupt I really am.*" Thus it is obvious these people simply don't want to practice a religion and in their request for God to prove themselves there is no possible outcome that requires them to practice a religion. So for them it's really not about whether there is a God at all, they just don't want to practice a religion so they eliminate the possibility of a God existing and will not accept a proof that would leave them alive to practice a religion. These people just aren't sincere so you should expose their insincerity in claiming to want to know the truth of it all. That's why I added that extra bit in the previous italics, because typically they play this game of "Draw God", "Make God speak, now" or "May I be struck down" with an audience present to overhear/observe. In private only the genuine idiots play such pathetic games, so with them you should be more gentle. In a public setting you have to remember you can preach to the audience without them knowing it by seeming to preach to an opponent, so if some cocky atheist plays this crooked game with you in public and doesn't want to stop when it's refuted then call them out and expose their insincerity so people aren't fooled by their attempts to seem fair/reasonable when denouncing religion/God. Even if their game with God results in just a severe injury then what? If God were to prove he exists by injuring them, then they would argue that they don't want to worship God because he hurt them and any God who hurts people to prove he exists is mean and forcing people to worship them. They'll say he is not a good God if he automatically hurts those who doubt his existence, even though that's what they asked for, because he's God he should've known better and proved himself in a different safer less harmful way. Also it wouldn't be sincere if the person is only worshipping God due to being hurt by God when God proves himself. Just tell such people who use this line of challenging God that God is not a bully and if God hurt you then you wouldn't want to worship God. They'd just be doing it out of compulsion and fear of more hurt. This infamous challenge of "*If God exists then may I be struck down*" is not a new challenge. This is exactly the same challenge people in the past gave to prophets. The people of Noah pbuh asked the same word for word and then they got struck down. Yet then the philosopher/atheist will say those are just stories, to which you can respond Hiroshima and Nagasaki weren't really bombed by atomic bombs either then, they are just stories on par with the destruction of Sodom. While if they insist that atomic bombings in the past were real then you can argue that if they were real then have the U.S. drop one on me right now to prove it, if they don't then it must not be real and must just be stories because if they did it to people in the past then they can do it to me now. If they don't do it to me now then they couldn't have done it in the past according to the "*If God exists then make him do X*" game. Therefore it all comes down to God not having to follow our orders. Besides if God were to send the exact sign that is requested what guarantee is there that when the person sees the sign then they'll believe it? Other people in the past asked for signs from prophets, got their signs and then still rejected the prophets despite getting the exact sign they asked for. So how do you know they will accept a sign from God if they get one? They'll say you can trust them to accept a divine sign when they get one. Yet how can they prove to you that they are smart enough to recognize one? Plainly tell them you think they are too stupid to recognize a divine sign when they get them. If they persist in their request then show them the signs God has already given to mankind and tell them now they have many signs so will they accept it or keep playing games? Just ask such people directly, "*If you get proof today are you willing to accept God's religion and practice it 100% and change your life or not?*" Ask them if they are willing to drastically change their lifestyle on the spot or not. If not then what's the point of them having proof if they aren't going to react correctly when they get it? Really what is the point of them getting proof? Why should God waste proof on such insincere corrupt creatures? Why should God give them special treatment when others don't get it and believe in him correctly regardless? Why can't they believe with the proofs that God already provided to mankind? Ask them if they really want proof of God and his religion, or if they just want an excuse to not believe in or practice any religion, or if they just say stuff to try to end the conversation about religion with them still seeming/feeling like they aren't a fool for not believing? Sincerely ask them "*Is there any possible way or anything I can possibly say that will cause this conversation to end with you accepting and joining my religion and following it strictly for the rest of your life? Or have you already decided you will never join my religion no matter what I say or what reasons/proofs I give you?"* Sometimes you just have to ask them where can the conversation go, it may still go places they never expect or desired but it can be good for you to learn about their sincerity level. Whether they are sincere or not you should still try and say what God wants but it's beneficial to ask such stuff, and for others who may be observing to know their answers to such questions. Our job is to obey God, not debate God. You will find that the person who wants God to prove themselves will typically never accept any proof. In reality they just want to make you feel less confident by not having the power to order God around at the behest of them and tend to only debate in order to seem smart or ridicule religion hoping to decrease the faith of the audience. By God not destroying them on demand it shows how wise God is, and this is why God created an eternal hellfire for people who play games like that. When God does start to punish them for arrogant disbelief, then God doesn't ever stop. So tell such people to wait because soon they will die and then they will see. They'll enjoy the wait and hope the topic is dropped, but when the game is over they'll regret it. The proof God is merciful is that God allows them to still live. Yet some of these types go to the grave with this belief, or make a deathbed change to believing that "a God exists" but still reject all religions. I witnessed one such deathbed religiosity where the philosopher who I've quoted throughout this book said on his deathbed: *"There must be some super-human type of being up there."* Then they told all our family that was present how they pray to God for us all every day. I thought it was funny how they believed a God existed just before they died, despite always giving me hassle for trying to get them to believe. Internally it was also funny to hear them say they prayed to God for me everyday when nearly every time I tried to talk to them about God they refused to believe a God even existed. I almost laughed at their blatant deathbed lies, but I didn't because my family would get upset if I laughed and exposed him on his deathbed. Unfortunately I forgot to ask him what proof God sent him that finally caused him to change his mind and believe in the baby-level faith that a God does exist, even though he commonly proudly claimed babies are born atheists. I guess it just took him his whole life to graduate to having a baby-level faith in a God. But as I said before a "baby-level" faith in a God existing is not enough to pass the test of life and enter paradise. Its amazing he refused to believe a God existed yet then "believed" in the possibility of a God with conviction minutes before meeting the angel of death. We are supposed to prove ourselves to God. God waits for us to prove we believe and are grateful, not to prove we are arrogant ingrates who simply don't want a God to exist so they play games that prevent themselves from practicing the true religion. No proof can ever be provided to the one who has already rejected what it proves. Ask the game player to prove they want proof and have sincerely tried to find proof on their own first. Demanding proof is very different from asking for proof. Some ask for proof, some just want to use a demand for proof as an excuse. Many who demand proof just prove they don't want it. One should be careful when asking for proof because once proof is provided you cannot reject it without suffering consequences. "The Proof" does not set you free, it enslaves you to the truth or your error. When the proof comes to you one thing is certain to occur, you will be a slave to something. Either the true God or a false god.

Believing in a god doesn't constitute a belief in God, it only means a person has a belief. Whether that belief is true or false, fact or fiction is more important, because everyone believes something. Believing in a god is the default human setting, Atheists just don't call their god a God. Having the correct belief about God is the determining factor in whether a human is functioning properly. We cannot customize God. God is the Creator of us, we have absolutely no right to create God. God has qualities so we can identify the true God from the false gods. Below are just a few.

The qualities of God

1. The one who created you and guides you.

2. The one who feeds you and quenches your thirst.

3. The one who heals you from sickness.

4. The one who will cause your death and give you life thereafter.

5. The one you hope will forgive your sins on the Day of Reckoning.

Just believing in the correct concept of God, which is beyond a "baby-level faith" or can be called "adult level faith" is not enough. Satan believes in God too. Satan even knows exactly what all the prophets pbut taught, he witnessed all they did and knows what is true regarding religion and what has been made up. Yet despite knowing with 100% certainty the truth about God, every prophet, every book of God and believing in God even to the extent that he has conversed with God (so he really really knows God well), Satan will spend eternity in hellfire. This is because having the correct belief is not enough, one must also obey, the part where Satan has gone astray is in his disobedience. Believing in God 100% correctly is just one part, if you rely on correct belief alone you are in the same boat as Satan. In fact Satan would be in a better boat because he knows a whole lot more information about God than you. The only way you could be better than Satan in the sight of God is if you obey God more than Satan, which again isn't as easy as it sounds since Satan worshipped God for over 4,000 years. He didn't do it until he died though so that is your opportunity to be better, if you do it til death. Obedience can only be achieved if we know what God wants us to do. Therefore Messengers have been sent in

38

order to give us those instructions we need to know of and follow in order to please our maker. Coincidentally these rules are good for us and protect us from all that is bad for us; it is a mercy from our maker that religious laws have been ordained. Now all the different religions have different laws and rules, some of which are contradictory, so no matter what you do you will be breaking the rules of one religion or another. Take sexuality for instance, should a man be celibate his entire life, or only have sex with a wife, or can he have sex anytime he wants married or not with any woman he wants, or can he have sex with other men married or not, what about sex with animals? The various religions all have a different position on sexuality and what sexual acts are good and evil, with each believing that if you don't follow their sexual rules then you are sinful. Likewise with eating, a Hindu considers a cow sacred and inedible, a Jew considers a pig unclean and inedible. If a Hindu ate a pig he'd think it's ok and if a Jew ate a cow he'd think it's ok yet they would both consider what the other was eating to be unlawful food in which the other is making God upset. The many differences between the religions means that people of different faiths are living opposite lifestyles of each other that are contradictory to the other parties' religious beliefs. If two cars were driving in opposite directions we would not think they would end up at the same destination, so we shouldn't think that way regarding people. The reason it matters what religion you have is because your religion will determine the lifestyle you have and the actions you do and abstain from. If all religions count then there can be no religious law, for if one says something is ok to do then it would be ok for all people to do and nothing would ever be wrong. The moral fabric of society would collapse as this idea would spread, and it has. All these different contradicting religious rules can't possibly all come from the one true God. Seriously consider the abject immorality, vice, corruption, oppression, sin and evil in the world today. If all these religions were true and those who follow them are living how God wants, then why is society so sinful and immoral and increasing in badness? If you believe that all religions are divinely inspired and correct then we should be living in the most moral time of all with society becoming more moral with every passing day. This alone is sufficient proof that a lot of religions out there are false ideologies. The falsest ideology of all is that all religions are true and pleasing to the Creator. Clearly we are not living in a moral plateau of human civilization, there is even a place in America known as "Sin city". I won't mention its official name because it's not the best spiritual environment to be in, I wouldn't want anybody to think of going there having learned its official name from me. Our species has become so sinful that the people of this city feel as though it's an honor to live in a city so notorious for sin that it is known by such a nickname. On top of that they promote the name "Sin city" because they have no shame. What kind of people are these who boast of living in a city of sin? Is the religion practiced in "Sin city" correct and leading to heaven too? Fortunately there is a criteria to help us identify the true correct religion. Following are a few of its traits.

The criteria of the True and Correct religion

1. It must be from God.

2. It must prohibit polytheism in any form and it must also forbid all that leads to worshipping anything other than the God which it came from.

3. It should not be self-contradictory.

4. It should preserve people's honor, properties, lives and offspring.

5. It should be a mercy to mankind and save us from our own injustices, weaknesses and deficiencies.

6. It should give guidance via God's law and the intention of that law. While also telling mankind of our origin and our final destination.

7. It should answer all questions and solve all problems.

8. It should call to noble character, truthfulness, generosity, morality and prohibit all types of bad conduct.

9. It should provide happiness for its adherents and be natural.

10. It should lead to truth and oppose all falsehood. While prohibiting all types of evil destructive ideologies, systems, practices and items.

11. It should agree with the message of all genuine prophets.

Sounds pretty good and many would likely agree a religion like that should be believed in and followed by everyone. Yet since one of the criteria is that it should agree with the message of all genuine prophets, who were sent by God, how do we know if someone was a genuine prophet sent by God? Well it turns out there are signs of prophethood, because obviously God is not going to send us a messenger without that messenger having some type of credible identification. Following are some qualifying indicators.

The signs of Prophethood

1. They should call to the worship of God alone and to the abandonment of worshipping other than God.

2. They should call people to believe in him and he should also practice what he preaches to them.

3. God gives him various signs or miracles that cannot be denied, disproven or replicated.

4. Their message should agree with the fundamental theology of the message of previous prophets.

5. They should not call others to worship himself, his race, his clan, his nation or anything aside from the Creator.

6. They should not ask others for any compensation for their message.

Religion is not a matter of opinion. Religion is a matter of what is true and what is false, of what is good and what is bad. Your personal belief has no impact on the facts. All religions are not equal and each must be examined for itself without prior prejudice. You cannot know whether your religion is true if it's the only one you know of. Likewise a person changing from one religion to another doesn't mean that their latest religion is true either. For example a Hindu becoming a Buddhist doesn't mean either one is true or false. Nor does a Jew becoming a Christian mean Judaism is false and Christianity is true. It could be that someone leaves one false religion for another false religion that could be more or less false than that which they had before. It could even be that someone leaves the true religion and adopts a false one; as Satan did. It's important to note that despite the many false religions, the true religion does exist. The idea that the existence of different opinions or values proves that none of them are true or superior is entirely absurd. Differences of opinions should raise the question *"Which is true?"* it shouldn't banish them all as being false, just because there's more than one opinion. Consider a multiple choice question on a test with 4 different answers to choose from. Let's say 4 people take the test and they each answer that question differently, everyone picked a different answer and all the answers have been selected. Now all the people think they got the question right to the exclusion of all the rest. Obviously they cannot all be right because they choose different answers, but under no circumstances could they all be wrong, one of them is definitely right. This is a simple concept to understand, but when we replace the word "answer" with "religion" and use a larger number than 4, even though it's the same exact principle Satan tries to confuse us and make us think that there is no correct religion because there are so many incorrect ones. This is exactly what Satan wants us to think and why he has worked so hard creating false religions. If there was the religion of God and the religion of Satan and we only had two clear cut options, it would be a far easier choice, just as a True or False question on a test is easier than a multiple choice question. The less options there are then the less ways one can go wrong. The more false religions there are the more confusing it is, especially if one learns about numerous false religions first consecutively one after another. If you studied 10 religions in a row and found all of them to be false, that could be discouraging for some people, particularly when Satan is whispering the entire time that all religions are false and that we should stop trying to worship God. This is why so many false religions exist; Satan wants as many roadblocks, detours and traps for us as possible. Satan wants us all to go to hell, but humans will never all agree to follow the same thing and as a species we are incapable of unanimity. If everyone tried to drive on the same road to hell there wouldn't be room and no one would end up driving anywhere at all. So Satan invests in as many roads to hell as he can to make it confusing and distract us all from the one road to paradise. For example when some people find out that their religious book is corrupted they will jump to the conclusion that, "*If ____ (their book) is corrupted then all the books are corrupted.*" This is another extremely ignorant notion that prevails amongst mankind. It stems from an initial arrogant reaction in thinking, "*Because I've been duped then that must mean everyone has been duped.*" Naturally we don't like to contemplate the idea that other people could have been right while we were wrong. Frequently when we realize we are wrong then we hasten to equalize the species and bring everyone else down to our level and label them wrong as well. It is very dangerous, unfair and unjust to do this. Imagine you are at a bookstore browsing a bookshelf loaded with books. If you pick up the first book on the shelf and find that its cover was blue and without looking at the rest to see what color they were, proclaimed: *"All books are blue!"*, you'd be a fool and publicly ridiculed. Likewise if the first book on the shelf you looked at was written by a woman, to then proclaim " *All books are written by women!"* without checking each book before speaking would be just as stupid and deserving of ridicule. Once again while the principle is exactly the same, people tend to act differently when it comes to religious books. If they discover that one, two, three or more were written by men, corrupted and changed from their original form, some people tend to foolishly claim that all religious books and/or religions are man-made. This is a dangerous idiotic statement to make, because the person hasn't researched all the religions or read all the religious books so they aren't qualified to make such a statement in the first place, that's why it's idiotic. Such a statement is dangerous because if one of those religious books and/or religions is divine, made by God and is flawless then by making the statement that all religions are false or man-made then you just criticized God and said that a man had made what God had made. Now if you came up to me and said that someone else wrote my book, I'd be rather upset and think *"Who the heck do you think you are to tell me I didn't write this book? I wrote it! Who are you and where did you get your information? What is your problem? Why do you hate me?"* Assuredly the reaction of God to such an insult that his book was man-made and his religion was flawed or false would be severe. Then imagine that the person making these claims didn't even read the book that they're saying this offensive stuff about! Personally that would really get someone ticked off if someone told an author they didn't write their book when the accuser hadn't even read it. The anger God must feel when people slander his revelations, prophets or religion is unimaginable, that's why such a blanket statement of disbelief is so dangerous. It's one thing to believe in a false religion, it's another thing to say the true religion is false. Although this is exactly what the people who make such blanket statements are doing. To utter such a statement is actually one of

44

the worst things, if not the absolute worst thing someone can possibly do. It is unjust to lump all religions in the same category, especially without having examined them. This is exactly what Satan wants people to do, it is sad to witness people fall for his trap so passionately. Aside from arrogance and willful ignorance, humans tend to be lazy creatures. When faced with the proposition of having to research every religion in depth and then potentially having to change one's lifestyle in order to follow the true religion, many people are intimidated even without Satan intimidating them. Then these people make statements such as, "there's no way to ever know the truth". By saying this they are actually saying that everyone is going to hell because it is impossible to tell the difference between the true religion of God and the religions of Satan. This is incorrect for many reasons. Right off the bat they tend to make it plural adding a "we" which is completely unjust. If a person says they'll never know that's one thing, but to have that person say that nobody on the planet will ever know the truth is outrageous! By these people making such statements in the plural form they are including you and I. They're saying that you + me + everybody will go to hell since we'll never know the truth. May God protect us from such Satanic thoughts and speech. This Satanic notion of despairing in ignorance is false because God wants us to worship correctly. God would never let the true religion permanently vanish. If it were corrupted then a new prophet would be sent. Deep down those who say, "there's no way to know" are simply trying to justify living sinfully and not changing their life or habits. Truthfully such an attitude shows they don't want to know the truth. They hope their ignorance will be an excuse to save them from hell and grant them paradise, because by their own biased standards they think they're good. Except their attitude betrays their laziness and lack of initiative to find out the truth. Unless such a person can overcome their arrogance they wouldn't practice the true religion even if it were presented to them on a silver platter. This is because knowing the true religion means responsibility and accountability. They don't want that so they say, "*there's no way to know the truth*" because they can't handle the truth. Typically that's why this type tends to reject the possibility of sacred scriptures or a book of God being available on earth to read today or ever. Satan makes some sinful people get so disturbed to read or learn that their false beliefs or sins lead to painful destruction and the hate of God that they stop reading because they didn't like what the book said about people like them. They expect a book from their Creator to say "*You are perfect! I love you no matter what! Everything you think and do is right because you are just so special and amazing! You are definitely going to paradise, no questions asked, no changes made and I'm going to let you party your life away on earth too without ever suffering or changing a single thing about yourself. I love all those you love and hate all those you hate, just as you always thought/knew/hoped.*" Since no books attributed to God say this they are disappointed, especially if according to God's book they or someone they like or things they believe in or do are labeled evil and threatened with disparaging vocabulary. Rather than remain objective, as they usually claim to be, they use their personal feelings/shock to reject a religion or a religious book instead of using legitimate scholastic reasons for doing so. Of course though most are smart enough or quickly learn that saying "*I don't believe in religions or scriptures because they make me feel bad about myself, tell me I have to change my beliefs/behaviors to be a "good person" and don't teach what I thought they should.*" is quickly and easily condemned by religious folk as being a pathetic excuse, they formulate reasons for their disbelief getting these reasons from others who formulated them having been in the same position before them. Or sometimes they even get their excuse for disbelieving in a divinely revealed religion or book from Satan himself, thinking it's their "common sense" not realizing that's Satan's two cents or Satan sense so to say. These people do the same thing I did in 1st grade with the subtraction problems which I didn't like and found hard to do (work with). Back then I changed the subtraction problems to addition problems and told the teacher "There are no subtraction problems. They're all addition. See all the problems are clearly addition problems, every single one of them is addition." I did this because I didn't want to do the subtraction the paper said to do, so I said the subtraction problems didn't exist and told the teacher himself that there was no subtraction (just as people say there is no special scholastically sound sacred scripture sent by the Supreme Creator). Yet I knew the teacher wouldn't fall for me just saying it didn't exist without a good reason, thus I came up with what I thought was a pretty good case for there "Not being any subtraction problems on the paper for me to do." Yet the teacher didn't let me get away with my game and let me get away with my biased accusations and distortions of the fact. The fact was there was subtraction on the paper even though I hated it and didn't want there to be because it was very difficult for me. Fortunately I learned a lesson when I was a kid playing games insisting there was no subtraction because of personal dissatisfaction with the mathmatical requirements given to me to complete to pass the class. Unfortunately some people today play the same game I played with math and subtraction, but do it with religion and divine revelation. When I played my game, I really believed I was going to get away with it and just pass through all of school forever and the rest of my life by making every subtraction problem into an addition problem and insisting, *"If there was a subtraction problem I would do it but I don't see any subtraction problems, and I've looked for them very carefully but they aren't there. It's not that I can't or don't want to do subtraction, if I saw them I could do them and would but they just aren't there for me to do so I don't have to do any. I don't know why other people seem to see subtraction problems on their papers, because I can't see any on mine."* I thought this plan was genius but my classmates laughed and told me it'd never work and I'm going to get in trouble if I try getting away with it. I told them I'm not trying to get away with anything, there just wasn't subtraction on my paper. They asked me if I just don't like subtraction and I insisted that I had no problem with it if it was there but it wasn't, and that while I might not like all types of subtraction I could/would still do it if it was there but no subtraction problems existed and I didn't know why my color-coded picture looked so messed up in comparison to their picture because I was as good at math as they were, if not better and doing all the math problems I came across right. I actually don't think I got a single addition problem wrong, yet my picture was wrong because I wasn't doing what I was supposed to be doing so I was wrong even though I could make a seemingly strong case that what I was doing was right. Just as many others who live life without religion can fool people into thinking they are moral/righteous and living a great life when in reality their life is messed up. Tragically though when I played my game with subtraction, nobody else let me get away with it and I stopped playing it, but the people who claim that no divine revelation exists and no religion is true keep on playing their game and what's worse is they get other people to believe and support their game-playing with God. Just as I needed a stern refutation from my teacher to stop playing, some of these people need a no-nonsense refutation to their attitude. Directly ask the people if they simply just don't like what the books or religions say/teach and that's why they don't believe in any divine books or possibility of a true religion. Be honest with them and tell them they can just say they don't like it so that's why they don't believe in it and they don't have to play games pretending they aren't but are actually sincere. A sincere person doesn't think there is no possibility for any book to be from God or for any religion to be true, unless they are sincerely stupid. Those truly are the only two options, they either aren't sincere or they are sincerely stupid and don't be afraid to tell them this because they think this about religious people, though they may not say it or they'll say it "out of care for you". The truth regarding the insincere "no scripture, no true religion" crowd is that they can't handle any type of religious truth which they don't like and they don't like learning about stuff they don't like either, which is why they won't read, listen to or view most religious propaganda and will refuse when offered to do so or when challenged to refute them. I actually have people like this in my family and even though I'm family they never read any of my books because they are afraid of religion and can't handle religious cognitive dissonance. Yet such types will have their excuses for not reading my book, like time constraints or different beliefs etc but in reality they are afraid of finding out the truth to be something other than what they currently believe/like. Everyone has this fear to some extent, and many religions inculcate this aversion towards learning about other religions but if it's a religion that prohibits one from reading religious material from others that's one thing, the thing I find unacceptable is the person who claims they don't believe in any religion but have this religious policy towards religions and religions books. This is why the only excuse they have is to insist there is "no way to know the truth" because they can't justify their intentional ignorance in any other dignified manner. Not only are they unable to handle the truth, but they can't even handle it if someone else learned the truth. If someone else found the true religion it would mean they are wrong and would have to change. But because they have already committed themselves to their current way of life they refuse to accept any possibility that they would have to change their lifestyle in order to enter paradise. This is why to them there is no true religion because there is no way they can see themselves changing their lifestyle. This stems from another pagan idea which comes from the famous phrase "*see no evil, hear no evil, speak no evil*" usually depicted by 3 mystical Japanese monkey idols. The phrase itself is satanic, leading us to think evil can only be done by our eyes, ears and mouth. The slogan also completely ignores our duty to do good in life. As it relates to the subject, these people "*see no truth, hear no truth and speak no truth*". They will put their fingers in their ears and cover their eyes if you bring the truth before them, most of their speech is wicked, vain, deceitful or just pointless jabbering devoid of benefit and they put their hand over your mouth if you try to enlighten them. Perhaps the 3 idolatrous pagan monkeys are a representative of these people, meant to display how they don't want to have anything to do with the truth; thus the artist depicted them as monkeys. Satan probably just gave humans a different interpretation, as he often does. This attitude that "*there's no way to ever know*" reveals that such people don't want to know how to please God, or else they would never utter such a statement. If they truly cared about the true religion and pleasing God they would want to know and be searching far and wide for the truth. Sadly I know too many people who hold this false misanthropic satanic attitude and its difficult to be around them or interact. Such pride as they possess (or as possesses them) can never listen to the voice of reason, nature or religion. Their voice is the only one they pay attention to or respect. Their entire religion revolves around their own personal opinion. Thus their motto is "*Well I think...*" and they believe that their opinion can be equated with every other opinion or evidence. To them everything in a religion must agree with what they think or else that religion is wrong because they believe they cannot be wrong about religion, even though they may claim they don't think that. For the vast majority of people when they say "*I think...*" concerning religion their thought has no merit or value because they don't have theological nor intellectual qualifications to have a valid religious opinion. Pride is not a credential, being alive does not mean one is qualified. Having a brain doesn't mean one can have their own religious opinion count, they can and will have their opinions but they have to realize the limited worth their opinions have. Just because it's "your opinion" shouldn't mean anything to you, if you ever think that "your opinion" is more right because it's yours then that is pride and blameworthy bigotry. So that's one thing regarding religion in that not every opinion is valued, religious thought is not democratic and each person's religious opinions are not equal nor do they carry any weight in an argument. You cannot give extra worth to your opinions just because they are yours and you think you are right. If you are right then you can prove it without saying "*I think*", but if you are wrong then typically your only and strongest proof in an argument will be "*I think...*". The true religion is not something derived from personal speculation, but the easiest false scripture to believe in is your own speculation. The next time someone tells you "*Well I think we'll never know.*" tell them that you don't think but you know for a fact that they did not think of that statement on their own, because it's been taught by a false Greek prophet for over 2,270 years. That doctrine of theirs is actually a religious creed. In the 3rd century BCE the philosopher Pyrrho taught this nonsense of "*We'll never know anything about anything.*" Except Pyrrho didn't stop at religion he committed to this philosophy on everything, from religion, to the universe, to animals, to history, to recipes, to science, to math, this guy taught that "*A persuasion of certainty is a manifest testimony of foolishness.*" meaning that if someone has any certainty about anything then they are a fool because Pyrrho said it's impossible to be certain about anything, even your own name or that anything is real including your memory. To Pyrrho if you thought you ate X for breakfast then you were a fool because you can't prove what you ate since your memory could be wrong and so could all the possible evidence you bring, whether you bring witnesses, video, pictures, crumbs, etc. To Pyrrho "*We can never be certain about anything, except that we'll never be certain about anything. However even this cannot be known.*" And his own philosophy proves itself to be wrong. Thus the extra quick way to refute the "We'll never know" wisecrack is to say "*Well how do you know that?! How can you prove that you or we will never know? Prove it to me! I dare you right now to prove that we will never ever know the truth about religion and that there is no way to know. Can you prove it? Seriously you don't want me to have blind faith in you, do you? Please prove to me that there is no way to prove a religion to be true. Prove it! If you can't prove that we will never know then your doctrine is unproven. Therefore nobody should ever believe that "We will never know" because there is absolutely no proof to base that doctrine upon. Basically that's just an anti-religious doctrine of a lazy stupid fool. You got no proof that there is no proof. You don't know how to even say what you don't know and what is unknowable or not. Simply put you don't know what the hell you are talking about but because you are a clever smart person you are pretending to have religion all figured out, because you don't want to admit you're clueless and are afraid that you don't know something you should and someone else does."* At the root cause such people are fundamentally afraid that smart as they are they've yet to find out the truth regarding religion, so rather than admit they are still searching they try to say there is no truth to find out. That way they don't seem/feel stupid/inferior for not knowing the truth. Although unfortunately this hardens their heart and some eventually just don't want to know the truth because they are enjoying life and the truth might require lifestyle changes. Thus they unknowingly copy an ancient pagan doctrine of never knowing the truth because they are afraid that the truth might hurt or that they won't recognize or believe in the truth once its proven to them. The reason they follow and believe their own thoughts then resort to saying *"there's no way to ever know until you die"* is because they aren't willing to believe that what they think about religion is wrong and that they have to change what they think and do in order to be right and good. They believe they are good already. Therefore this means if they didn't know the truth that would mean they are bad, and they are smart enough to know their ignorance of the truth would mean they are bad, so to assure themselves they are good they have to believe that there is no religious truth which they don't know or believe in. Hence to be good and smart without a religion they have to reject religion altogether or else admit they might not be smart or good and they certainly won't do that unless of course everyone else is stupid and bad too. They will accept being labeled stupid and bad but only if everyone else is dumber and badder than they are. Of course they won't preach this, except as an excuse to stop someone else from preaching to them and nix religious conversations while seeming smart. Yet on the face of it by them saying nobody can ever know they are flat-out saying you are an idiot for thinking we can. These people are clever though and will condescendingly try to make you feel like the villain who should "bow to their wisdom and experience" instead of being a "fanatical zealot". So if they ever feel offended when you preach to them just ask them who has the greater right to be offended, them saying the truth is unknowable and people who think they know are stupid idiots or you saying that you know the truth and they don't. Truly their anti-preaching statements are more offensive when you analyze it and at the core level you are trying to make them a better more spiritual person and they are trying to reduce your religiosity and by extension morality. So fundamentally this *"Don't preach to me about religion."* doctrine is a very wicked immoral statement. Really what the hell are people supposed to talk about to become better? Without religions there is no morality, that is a fact. To have no religion in your conversations is immoral and destroys the very morality of the conversationalists. Never fear offending these people by talking about religion with them, they truly need it even though they'll angrily say they don't want it. Spiritually they've committed suicide. Their "smarts" and pride has killed their soul and if they die with such an unhealthy soul they'll cry blood from their eyes in hell wishing that you had spoken to them despite their anger. Yet regardless of this reality their pride makes them willing to die without a faith hoping to finally find out 100% how all those religious folk were stupid just like they said. Their god in this life is their opinion, their prophet is their arrogance. Sadly many of them prefer to die rather than accept the fact that their opinion is of no worth when it comes to religion. This is because to them dying is easier than disqualifying their personal opinion, they value their pride over their life and arrogantly prefer to lose their life before their pride. In short they think their thoughts about God and/or religion are divine revelation but think everyone else is just fooling themselves and others, except for them being the exception to the masses who make mistakes regarding their thoughts about religion(s). Their attitude of mankind's perpetual ignorance of what religion is true being "the religious truth" saddens me because it is the same attitude as the people who go to hell. They even hope they're right and want everyone to go to hell with them. Seriously they would rather be right about all religions being false and have there be no paradise than for them to be wrong and go to paradise. Their pride in their philosophy is their paradise. They religiously don't want to know of a true religion so they teach themselves a doctrine of ignorance being a fact because they desire their own religious ignorance to be okay with God, since for it not to be okay with God would mean they'd have to accept their current selves as a "religious fool" in need of divine guidance to know what is right and that hurts their ego. In short they don't want to learn what's right because it hurts their feelings too much to accept that they are wrong in the present and need to learn what's right before being right. Such people are nearly unteachable when it comes to religion because they think that if someone else knows more about a true religion then by default it makes them better because they mistakenly think God favors the knowledgeable over the sincere/pious. Whereas just because someone may know more than you doesn't automatically mean they are better. Their opinions may be worth more but to God they may be worth less due to their own personal or spiritual defects that are known to God alone. Sadly Satan has fooled the ignorant people into thinking their ignorance means God hates them when God's hatred only comes from their choice to be ignorant not their ignorance itself. By not admitting and acting like an ignorant person they become sinful and hated by God, but ignorance itself does not merit hate unless the ignorance is inexcusable or chosen in opposition to the truth. The sin of ignorance is in the ignoring of the truth or the path to the truth God sent his prophets with.

Rather than accept their religious ignorance and humbly seek the answers with an intention to follow them, this agnostic type of disbeliever thinks they are born right or at the least are currently right about the true religion being unknowable so they reject the possibility of the right answers being known by others solely because they can't accept their own errors. They are enslaved to the pride of their own ignorance. They can't be guided because they think it's too embarrassing to let God guide them. Although their being alive gives me hope in the mercy of God, because God is so merciful he allows these people to still enjoy so many blessings despite their aversion to worshipping him correctly. Since they haven't yet died there is still a chance that God will guide them and rectify their condition, if they are willing to repent and submit to their Creator. May God help us to be grateful. May God help us strive to learn and accept the truth whatever it is, wherever it is, regardless of our condition when it comes to us or whoever/however we learn it. If one doesn't know the true religion, then they don't know how to get to heaven and if they don't know how to get to heaven then how do they expect to live there? If according to them they "*will never know the truth*", then it follows that they will never enter paradise. If a person isn't entering paradise then there is only one other option, may God protect us from it. A person who says there is no true religion is saying all religions are false. Now despite all the different religions contradicting each other making it impossible for them all to be true there is one absolute truth that they all agree upon. The truth all religions agree upon is that at least 1 religion is true. Therefore the person who says all religions are false is a disbeliever according to every single religion in the world. This means that someone who believes and says that there is no true religion has absolutely 0% chance of going to paradise if they die with that belief, this is something every single religion agrees upon. So for that person it doesn't even matter what religion is true because they automatically rejected it. This is the most evil type of belief one can have, because such a person rejects the possibility of paradise and is practically trying to go to hell. If you choose 1 religion the rest may say you're going to hell because of it but at least there is a theoretical logic that says that if you were right then you'd go to paradise. But the one who says there is no true religion is essentially trying to go to hell according to every religion. A person who worships a piece of feces is better than the one who says all religions are false. This is because at least the feces worshipper believes in the concept of worship. Religion teaches you how and what to worship, the one who says all religions are false is saying that nothing is worth worshipping in any way. Of course some people say they worship God in their own way but just not according to any religion, these people are turning themselves into prophets thinking they can teach themselves how to worship God even though the real prophets themselves had to be taught by God how to worship. Some just don't want to be taught but soon God will make them learn in this life or the next. However in the next life you will get the results for your test of life. So imagine what an awful result the person who starts learning after their life is over is going to get on the test of life? The one who waits until they're dead to find out the truth and believe it, is exactly like the kid who waits until after the exam is over before they register to take the class. Will that person pass? No, they will burn in hell for being both a fool in practice and in theory. Stupidity hurts, it hurts a lot, and religious stupidity hurts a lot for eternity.

What about the religion of Science? Is Science a religion? Well it depends. "Exact Science" is the quantitative treatment of data. That's not a religion, that's statistical. While "Pure Science" is the deductive operations from self-evident principles. That's logic and sometimes philosophy so it can be a religion. Then "Natural Science" is the observation and experimentation with natural phenomena. That's not a religion it's just observation and experimentation. However typically "Science" as it's practiced tends to be practiced in the order of "Natural Science" followed by "Exact Science" then "Pure Science" creates doctrines due to "scientific principles", often called theories or laws. That last bit of science can be religious and bigoted as well as contradictory to Natural and Exact sciences. Some types of "Pure Science" is unscientific. The "Evolution theory" is one such type of unscientific creed that poses as scientific fact, but to think it's fact is a matter of faith that actually is proven false by Natural Science. Yet due to the power "Pure Science" dogma has over people many confuse the religion of Science with the application of scientific study or experimentation. Science becomes a excuse for religious beliefs which many people believe are proven facts due to some "scientists" claiming it, oftentimes incorrectly I might add, or due to non-scientists misunderstanding the actual statements/studies of natural or exact science. Basically not all "science" is scientific or secular. Originally science was a type of philosophy and philosophy was a type of science, but as science became more involved with the physical instead of the abstract, immaterial and spiritual then modern peoples forgot the connection to the extent that many consider philosophy and science to be separate not realizing they are synonymous in many ways. Science is in essence a philosophy for studying the material world and it's operations. The primary aim of science is explanation, and that explanation has a definite meaning, this is also one of the main aims and effects of religion. The task of science is to explain phenomena by defining them strictly, ordering and classifying them, then relating them logically to other data and other logical explanatory structures within the realm of science. Replace the word science in the previous sentence with religion and you will see how science can be and in a very real sense is a religion. The religion of "Pure Science" only uses it's own sources and rejects outside philosophies or explanations as unuseable to the scientific realm, even if those come from the realm of natural science or exact science. Scientific findings that contradict popularly held doctrines of "Pure Science" tend to be denounced as unscientific heresies despite being accurate science who's only "error" is that it proves certain "scientific theories or laws" to be false and contradictory to natural science. So you have science the methodology and science the philosophy. Then you have empiricism which is an entirely different philosophy which many confuse as being science. Empiricism is the philosophical religion that man can have no knowledge of the universe that is not a consequence of perception and experience. You remember the philosophers who say they want to see or hear God or else he doesn't exist? They are empiricists. They foolishly believe if humans can't perceive something then it must not be real, because otherwise people would know about it. Why? Because they think humans are the top life form in the world. Empiricism is intellectual racism thinking the perception of the human race determines reality. However technically no definition of empiricism is correct because every human perception differs, so what empiricsm is to one or many is not nor can it ever be the same to all because all have different levels of perceptions. That is the absurdity of empirical thought. It's something that can't even be defined because according to empirical definition our perceptions (which are the only reliable authenticator) are all different and have different standards for definitions due to unequal abilities of perception. Just imagine if any other creature believed that the only truth in the Universe was what it's race or it individually perceived. If any creature that only lived on Antarctica were empiricists this would mean they would say that only Antarctica exists and nothing else does. Honestly empiricists are the same type of people who believed the earth was flat because obviously human perception says its flat, *"Can't you tell without anyone telling you?"* Does walking or running on earth feel like you are running on a moving sphere? Only after getting pics from space could an empiricist possibly believe earth was not flat. The Empiricst motto is basically

"Nobody needs to be told, our senses tell us everything and all we need to know can be known through our senses, reality is nothing other than what we perceive it to be." Empiricism is nothing but human arrogance and it's so easy to refute if you simply know how. If deep sea fish were empiricists then all that is on land could not be believed to exist since they don't perceive it. If trees were empiricists they'd have to disbelieve in all the tales of deep sea creatures and corals. For the empiricists who claim *"I won't believe it until I see or hear it."* then just tell them how its good that glasses and hearing aids are around because otherwise they might have to stop believing the truth if their eyesight got worse or they lost hearing. An empiricist would have to stop believing in the seen world if they ever went blind because to them reality is perception. Human memory is known to be faulty so they can't claim that memory is the same as perception. Also they can't just "blindly follow" the advice of the seeing about the seen world such as various colors being real because that's not perception if you just believe what you are told about the perception of others. Empiricists proudly claim not to believe anything unless they have proof or observe it, however to not believe anything without perception means one must disbelieve in it without perception, which means disbelieving in what is true simply because of human flaws in perception. If humans cannot perceive everything that exists then an empiricist can never believe in everything that exists. They may cheat and use technology to justify belief in invisible or imperceptible things but even with technology there is a limit to what humans will ever be able to perceive. Humans will never be able to perceive or observe every facet of the universe, but it still exists and operates despite us not perceiving it whether we believe it or not. Empiricists are like the kids who said they don't believe in Santa Claus because they never seen him. Whereas perceiving Santa with the sight, smell, taste, touch or sound doesn't determine whether he is real or not. Santa Claus could still exist even if nobody can see, smell, taste, touch or hear him. Empiricists technically have no valid reason to not

believe in Santa Claus unless they find other proof to prove a conspiracy or the impossibility of the myth and contradictions within it. I'm not saying Santa exists, he doesn't but to say it's wrong to disbelieve in Santa simply due to a lack of perception of him is an invalid argument to make. Yet they make this argument with God, despite the non-empirical proof that Santa Claus doesn't exist not applying to the case of God. Basically for an empiricist to believe in God they'd have to perceive God and since to fully perceive God, a superior being, in all his majesty you'd have to be God then the empiricist cannot believe in God unless they are God or they stop being a foolish arrogant empiricist who thinks collective human perception is the epitome of the knowledge of the universe. Why do people believe in empiricism? Typically because they don't trust people as individuals for personal reasons and trust issues. To avoid trusting individuals who are unworthy of trust in their opinion, or "blindly following" as they'd put it, they adopt the Satanic doctrine that collective human perception is the standard of truth and that "proof" is perception. Thereby they become easy targets for Satan who as a Jinni is not perceived by them and can play with them however he pleases with them being cluelessly manipulated. Yet even their doctrine of perception being proof contradicts itself. The prophets perceived God so God must exist then, especially since so many others also perceive and observe God's influence throughout the world. The empiricst then must label the perception of religious humans as defective but under what pretenses? Simply because they don't want to believe in a religion and follow the rules of God for life. For many it always comes down to that, not wanting to follow God's rules. If it were just to believe in a God and that's it then they'd have no problem with believing in God or a religion, but it's because of the rules of God that they have an issue with religions and God existing. Their issue is usually with existence because to admit existence means to admit rules must exist, which they must/should follow which allows criticism and potential failure/condemnation by people as well as punishment if they don't or won't. So they deny God's existence by denying the validity of the perception of God amongst those who believe in God and insisting their own human perception is the deciding factor. Yet they don't take this approach with other things in life, such as the flatness of earth. They trust an astronaut not to fake a picture or misperceive earth but they refuse to trust a prophet or religious folk who perceives God. Why? Because the astronaut doesn't come to them with a rulebook. If the astronaut told them because Earth is not flat you have to do XYZ until you die, the empiricist would say earth was flat and the astronaut was just a liar or deluded trying to control them and that human perception dictates earth is flat so it is and it's foolish to think otherwise just because some astronaut "who went to the heavens and back" says he perceived something and came back with some signs from the heavens as "proof". An Empiricist wouldn't believe in a prophet unless they were the prophet and perceived what the prophet perceived or the miracle the prophet came for people to perceive. However the truth is such that you don't need to perceive what a prophet perceived or a miracle to believe in it and its known that perception as well can be rejected by humans since many who did witness actual miracles rejected them. Spiritually the empiricists are blind, deaf and dumb and can't perceive their own arrogance and feeblemindedness. They've fallen for the scam artist Satan by thinking following human perception was the way to never get religiously scammed. They were scammed due to a fear of getting scammed. In short they vastly overestimate the human species and tend to rely on science incorrectly thinking/claiming it is the same as empiricism. To teach them one should begin by explaining how stupid and imperceptible man is to the world. The senses of animals are well-known to be superior to our own. So if empiricism was true then animals must know better than us about the universe since they perceive more. Only a fool can be an empiricist, the hard part is teaching such a fool how to perceive their foolishness. You can ask them if a human can't perceive they are stupid and clueless does that mean they aren't? If nobody can perceive a person is sick, smart or insane does that mean they aren't? How can you perceive that human perception is reliable/trustworthy? People hallucinate all the time for many reasons. It's entirely possible that you see, hear, taste, smell and touch something and perceive it to be God but does that mean it is God? Verily the majority are ignorant so the perception of the majority cannot be trusted but then what of the majority of our senses? How do you know life isn't all just a dream? Because human perception is not reality. That's why so many marriages and relationships fail because they perceive love or friendship when they don't really have love or friendship. Since humans are prone to error for innumerable reasons then human perception is prone to error as well and cannot be the only proof accepted as to what is the truth. Just as the past cannot be known by human perception alone neither can the truth. To only accept human perception or observation as a proof of the truth is to be no different than animals who follow nothing but their instincts and senses. In reality though this is what empiricists believe, that we are all animals which simply evolved thus no religions are needed or real. Thus they appeal to science and try to use the credentials of science to back up their unscientific nonsensical religious methodology. Much of the mainstream "scientific world" is influenced and believes in science the philosophy or empiricism but claims its just a method that has nothing to do with religion. These scientists forget that science seeks to establish relationships not "understanding". Science is about connecting dots not about fully explaining what the dots are/mean or how/why they connect. Science is an academic tool not a source of knowledge, science does not provide answers it only reveals potential relationships. A "scientific explanation" asserts that on the basis of knowledge already in our possession, certain phenomena (those to be explained) are to be expected. Reread that, that is what science is. It is an assertion about the expected occurrence of certain phenomena, which is to be explained by some other source of knowledge that is not science. Unfortunately many think science is the explainer when it is just the assertor useful for drawing relationships that could be true or false. To give "science" a monopoly on answers/explanations is unscientific and causes disaster. Again science is a tool to be used by the knowledgeable not a toolchest with all types of knowledge contained within it. Scientific constructions are human creations, not discoveries. If one purports that "Science explains X" then they must answer which type of the 6 recognized explanations is that particular explanation? First there are Probabilistic Explanations, explained by reference to probabilistic generalizations, not universal, in which tendencies can be used. But in reality that's a generalization based on generalizations nor an explanation in the sense in which most understand the word as being "the true/correct answer". Next are Causal Explanations which explain singular events by specifying the antecedent conditions that are necessary and/or sufficient to generate the event. But since that's just cause and effect it's unknown how reliable/accurate that is since it is extremely easy and common to misattribute causes to certain effects AND frequently the causes that lead to effects in the past can never be repeated because for the cause to happen a 2nd time is impossible because the same exact thing cannot ever truly happen 2 different times within one timeline. Nothing in the Universe ever happens twice, everything is unique with specific specialties distinguishing it from all other events. Hence since no 2 effects are ever alike then no 2 causes can ever be alike especially since any 2nd cause would be in many ways effected by the first similar cause that took place earlier in the timeline. Technically there is 1 original cause and everything that follows is an effect of the thing that got everything started. Religious folk would say God was the cause and everything else that ever happens is an effect of God causing the initial cause of everything else, so that all "causes" are just effects of the 1st cause (God). But to say "because of God causing the initial cause" isn't a very satisfying explanation for most things for most people. Don't mistake that for thinking God just got the ball rolling and had nothing to do after the initial Cause chain-reaction occurred, God is always involved in every cause and effect, past present and future, but while being the cause of all that doesn't make him responsible for everything. For example we are the cause of the effect of eternal hellfire but despite God creating both us and hell God is not the cause or reason people will burn in hell. Why? Because they could have avoided that and went to paradise if they obeyed. Just like how your boss is the one who fires you and is the "cause you got fired" in reality you are the true cause of being fired due to your own incorrect beliefs/actions or lack thereof. Anyways Causal explanations are circular and futile since every cause always has a cause until one must acknowledge something must eternally have existed without a cause before it, and then that causes people to believe in God, scientifically according to Causal explanations. Yet the mainstream science faith claims science teaches otherwise. Thirdly is Functional Explanations which use expressions related to particular phenomenon to the system it occurs in. These are technical explanations involving specialist terminology invented solely to describe what could not be described/referred to without functional vocabulary. Basically this is when scientists make up words for stuff, pretending those words are explanations. Much of this is just Jargon which laymen don't understand not because they are laymen but because those using the terms don't really have an explanation but have to say something for the sake of communication and sharing information. Fourthly there are Teleological explanations which identify the purpose or goal that particular events fulfill. Science can provide some of these but many times the cult of science advertises mere hypothetical theories as teleological explanations when they aren't. At the end of an experiment each experiment only works once, to redo any scientific experiment in reality is to do another experiment. You cannot replicate an experiment, you can do another that is very similar but every experiment is always different so even with the teleological explanations identification of purpose is in many regards theoretical past on past events. Yet as any good investor knows "Past results are NOT indicative of future results." The past by itself is not very trustworthy, especially since the past is irrepeatable. Fifthly there are Genetic Explanations which trace the past history of a single event, presumably to a point where the inquirer understands how the event came to occur. Yet with these it's impossible for our species to ever know every variable and true cause unless one who can know every variable and the entirety of history informs us of the real how of an event. Especially when people in the present don't have 100% access to the past, even if they lived it, so every variable can not be known by any creature known. So these either come from God or are technically invalid explanations. Sixthly science has Deductive Explanations. A Deductive explanation has 4 components to it. 1. A general empirical law or universal generalization. 2. A statement of conditions under which the generalization holds true. 3. Event to be explained 4. Rules of Logic. However the key element of deductive explanations is that universal generalizations are necessary. Empirical laws are universal generalizations. Without universal generalizations deductive explanation is impossible. In summary with all these 6 types of scientific explanations science is primarily educated generalizations. There is never 100% certainty with scientific explanations and exceptions that break the "laws of science" abound. Every miracle is an example of such "law breakage" thus proving the fragility and impermanence of scientific law. And that applies to everything, earth can stop spinning, it could grow or shrink. The scientific laws of the universe in theory can always change in an instant making all that science has said or thought to be wrong. Learning is irregular and unending so individuals and organizations constantly change as they learn. Thus science constantly changes too. The laws of science change, so do the principles and methods. Now if the rules, principles(beliefs) and methods of something perpetually changes we'd say that's a false faith. Hence science in some respects is much like a false faith, it's just a tool but if taken as a philosophy and answer to life then it is a faith whether it's adherents think or claim it is or not. Science therefore is different things to different people. For some it can be their religion and for others it can be a tool. Yet does this classification of science disrespect the many scientific theories? Not if you know what a "theory" is. Theories may explain but can never predict. Theories can explain or relate generalizations. Theories are simply instruments for ordering and arranging statements that man creates for his own purposes and not in any way are they a map or picture of "reality". Theories are not facts, they could be true but they can never be considered as facts. Now what types of theories exist?

Hierchical/Deductive theories: Used if/when a relationship is deductive and the general statements in the theory are logical derivatives of a few basic axioms or postulates.

Concatenated theories: Used if general statements in theory are not related deductively but held together by some other factor like relevance to a common class of phenomena.

Quasi-theories: Any intellectual construction that is useful but cannot meet the standards of deductive or factor theories.

A theory, whether scientific or otherwise, is a generalization or set of generalizations that explains general statements or other theories. Theory construction is a continuous cumulative enterprise. Theories grow by modification, accretion and occasional contributions. Theories by definition are not facts. Likewise possession of facts is not knowledge, because facts must be related to each other or else they are useless and incomprehensible due to their randomness. Knowledge is true, beneficial, readily comprehended, comprehensive and transmittable. Theories are transmittable or comprehensive but can be more difficult to comprehend and more importantly they can be false or of negative effect. Facts are true, transmitted, and comprehensible but of very little benefit if they are gathered into theoretical format or not in the format of knowledge. Facts are reference points used to prove a greater construct, alone facts prove very little and their benefit is negligible and they can even be dangerous if not digested wisely or if one's awareness of facts is incomplete or sporadic. Think of facts as though they are numbers in a mathematical equation. Numbers are integral to mathematics but with organization and relationships to other numbers, mere numbers by themselves are useless and can even be dangerous if misunderstood/misinterpreted, misconveyed or abused. Anyways theories are not technically classifiable as knowledge because they are in the informational classification of speculation, theories can benefit in similar ways as knowledge does but theories are not knowledge though both may produce similar effects. Anyways theories grow hoping to officially become knowledge one day or be rejected as falsehood, yet in the meantime they are simply theories that are not knowledge and can be either pure speculation or a useful intelligently crafted likely yet unproven probability/inference. This is why scientific theories commonly build upon other scientific theories, which leads the referenced theories to become more credible but this phenomenon of theories building upon theories instead of authentic undisputed knowledge therein causes the problem of the religion of science. In Islam we'd say science doesn't always base it's aqeedah or fiqh on sahih information but uses all types, including weak, forged, misrecorded, mistakes, bias, political/economic/personal desires. In the rules of argument, for those who know how to argue correctly, an argument or explanation is impossible until the standards of evidence have been defined and agreed. This is because "logical truth" is absolute. For it is utterly impossible to accept premises and refuse the conclusions of a logical argument except through self-contradiction. This is why with the purveyors of falsehood if you allow them to start a debate based upon false premises, such as using unscholastic methods or by using unauthentic/unproven information one has fundamentally already given them victory by letting them flee the battlefield of facts and allowing them to fight you in a realm where fantasy or speculation is accepted as referenceable/useable. It's still possible to win and refute a purveyor of falsehood on their home turf but methodologically it is unsound, unwise and dangerous for the majority of people to do. Yet regarding theories, by definition a theory is something that is not agreed upon by any legitimate authority because if it was then it wouldn't be a theory it would be knowledge. So regarding argumentation and explanation, scientifically no theory can be justifiably used as a building block for other theories because theories are still speculation no matter how educated a speculation they may be, a speculation is not a fit foundation to work with. Nor can a scientific theory be safely, scientifically or justifiably taught unless the scientists/teachers specify everytime to every member of their audience that it is a theory and "unproven/potentially false". Yet how many scientists/teachers will specify when they teach/debate/explain that every theory they use/discuss/reference is "unproven/potentially false". Nearly none, and certainly not the school teachers unless you are at an extremely academically advanced scholastic level. Thus science is methodologically unsound and unscholastic, useful though it may be and true as some elements of it may be. For example if theory A is wrong but scientists don't know its wrong yet then make their case for theory B being true based on the acceptance of theory A and they do the same for all the other theories in the scientific alphabet, if/when A is proven wrong that means all the theories that used A may well be wrong so belief in theories B-Z must be suspended and labeled unjustified because theory A was wrong and influenced the formulation of all the other theories. Frequently throughout history theories, scientific and otherwise, are debunked/rejected and new theories have had to be formed starting back at the foundational level. So with science you have a system where if anything is ever wrong and popularly accepted as right, which has happened a lot as scientists admit, then to make things right many things, if not everything, that science has "found out" after theory A and theorized due to belief in theory A being true, must be rejected until proven right without A or anything based upon A. Regarding religion this would be like saying Christianity is based on the bible and then finding out the bible was not the word of God nor written by anyone who actually met Jesus pbuh. This would disqualify the bible and anything based off of it and if the bible were debunked/rejected and Christianity were based off of it then belief in Christianity would need to be suspended until extra sources were found to support it and if those sources/theories were not found then belief in Christianity would need to be scrapped simply because the biblical building block was debunked/rejected and unusable. As it relates to science this means if scientists 500 years ago made a mistake about a theory then we found out today they made a mistake, for the sake of intellectual integrity the last 500 years of scientific research would have to be scrapped and rejected as wrong and science would have to start over from square one or at the least suspend belief in all the scientific data and theories that used the building block of the now known to be erroneous 500 year old theory. Of course many scientists don't want to do that since it could mean technological downgrades and a loss of reputation for the subject of science in general, but if the foundation blocks of theories are invalid then the whole scientific infrastructure is unstable, untrustworthy and unreliable until proper foundations are set to support the later theories. Thus either people find the truth out real soon to avoid rejecting much of science, or they cling to erroneous theories for the sake of keeping the top blocks of science intact and esteemed though they should be discarded or temporarily put aside and unused for the sake of intellectual integrity. When people are willing to restart scientific research from the ground level when a core/base theory is proven wrong this is good and healthy science. When they don't then science is a false religion, ineffective, unscientific and loses credibility as a whole because the pillars that support it are mythical/erroneous and scientists really don't know why things work or are the way they are but don't have the guts to admit the later/modern theories have no foundational theories to support them. Religion used to be able to fill the occasional gaps in science so science could credibly not have the answers for some foundational theories by using/borrowing those theories from religions. Although after people started to reject religion and all religious rules in exchange for freedom, to keep science alive with credibility the false doctrines and debunked theories have to be presented as truth until a suitable replacement explanation can be found. Basically many scientists simply fake it as being factual until they figure out why it is, or find out a different formula if to replace the false doctrine they've been fibbing for. Most scientists don't have the guts to say *"theory A was wrong so although theories B-Z could be true we don't as of yet have any good justifiable reason to believe B-Z since theory A which led us to formulate B-Z is wrong"*. However not every scientist knows that for credibility purposes many pretend false theories are true and continue to teach what they know is wrong until they find out what the truth really is. Yet this is why many in the mainstream science cult believe in unscientific things like the evolution theory, which has been thoroughly debunked by scientists for the sake of scientific integrity because it's unscientific and impossible, yet the reason it gets taught despite scientists proving it false is because other potentially true science is built upon it. The masses like answers so many insincere teachers would rather teach something wrong to give people an answer rather than admit they don't know something or can't explain why something is the way it is or why something works. The Evolution theory is wrong according to science but it's taught today for 2 reasons. 1. Because people don't want to say they don't have a explanation for human origins without agreeing with Creationism and thereby validating religion. 2. People and ignorant pseudo scientists think evolution is right because they heard it preached to them and believe in the science that evolution is built upon, even though that later science in reality is valid despite evolution being invalid but currently it can't be explained or accepted as 100 % valid without referencing evolution which is invalid. Thus to escape religious explanations mainstream science validates and preaches invalid unscientific theories for the sake of scientific potentially valid theories as well as other invalid theories too, but in the long term this leads many to incorrectly reject those valid and potentially valid theories thinking they are invalid due to their fraudulent links and reliance upon invalid theories. For now the mainstream science cult is popular but if it keeps playing this deceptive game eventually the cult of science will discredit the tool of science as the cult members take over the tool and use it ineffectively due to accepting invalid theories which will lead to invalid science eventually. The dishonesty of some scientists not only risks the reputation of science but the very progress and usefulness of it. Why take that risk? Because certain false religions in the past outlawed science so many scientists fear using religion as the foundational block filler and complement to things science can't explain yet, or ever, lest the religious try to outlaw science again should religion become popular. Basically scientists are afraid to be honest for the sake of reputation and because of past oppression by certain false religions who opposed scientific progress for various reasons some religious and some political and some just crazy/stupid. Science was institutionally abused in the past and that past abuse has led it to develop unhealthy unscientific habits as a security measure, but these habits are negative not just for science's sake but the sake of our species, intellectual progress and technological advancement. The pride of science is discrediting it scientifically and in the eyes of many religious people who are less familiar with science and the pride of the cult of science is holding true natural and exact science from reaching it's potential to benefit us all. The popularity and influence of the cult of science backfires and is now turning the tool of science into a false religion and philosophy. Yet many religious unscientific people and unreligious members of the mainstream cult of science think it's a battle between "Religion VS. Natural/Exact Science" when it's something else entirely. To be fair the false religions all do have a problem with Natural/Exact science but Islam doesn't and the true religion by definition can't. However the cult of science is incompatible with the truth. Anyways Science, whether the fake mainstream faith of Science or true Science, is merely a human construct and can be criticized as well as rejected because it's simply a man-made tool. To think everything scientific is good and everything unscientific or anti-scientific is bad/wrong is to make science, even true science, a religion where the scientists are the prophets. "Being Scientific" means being scientific, and that's all it means. It doesn't mean that "being scientific" means you are smart or right or superior. It's like saying someone is athletic, athleticism is simply a tool that can be good or bad, right or wrong. Some people are too athletic and some people are too scientific, while others worship athleticism and some worship scientificity. A "scientific result" or a "scientific approach" is not inherently better or correct. To think such is to view science, even true science, as a religion instead of a methodology. To "be scientific" is to have a prejudiced view that is intolerant of other viewpoints and methodologies. That's really what being scientific means, it means you are prejudiced with a scientific bias towards life. Prejudice is not inherently evil but rather than have any scientific prejudice we are supposed to have prophetic prejudice. A scientific mentality or approach is different than the prophetic mentality and approach, so beware of science so that it doesn't become too important in your life. Many people are extremists when it comes to science and are either too scientific or not scientific enough, the test of life is complex. Personally since science, whether genuine or the cult, can be and function as a religion with scientists becoming near clerical in prestige and influence I believe there should be a separation between Science and State. Neither the cult of Science nor genuine Science should have the type of influence it currently has on global governments. Scientists may fear such talk from a religious person but in truth during our modern era science has overstepped itself. At the minimum the unscientific mainstream cult of science should not be promoted by the State as it currently is by many states. They promote the pseudo-science cult and its doctrines simply because it helps the economy, weakens morality, inculcates anti-religious outlooks and neuters citizens by encouraging patriotism + discouraging rebellion. What is the creed of the cult of science or pseudo-science?

1. *"I believe that life has no special purpose or meaning. The same is true for the entire universe. Nothing has any "special purpose"."*

2. *"I affirm that my and all morals come from genes and social conditioning, not from decisions that I make. Freewill is an illusion. My personal identity and/or "soul" is a fictional myth."*

3. *"There are no "good" deeds or any "good people". There is no "bad", "evil" or "wrong" either. People + deeds are equal/neutral."*

4. *"Every report of encounters with spirits, angels, ghosts, demons, Gods, Heaven or Hell or anything supernatural is all fiction and stupid superstition. It can never ever be credible no matter what."*

5. *"I am my physical brain and nothing more. The death of my body is the death of me. There is no afterlife nor a God. Death ends all."*

Many people with some integrity have a conscious that tells them this isn't true and they would never teach this credo, but this is fundamentally exactly what mainstream science teaches. They just use eloquent vocabulary and indirect indoctrination techniques to subtly preach these doctrines. Take point #1, that life is meaningless. Most scientists won't say this but it's what science today is forced to teach because if our life does have a purpose then what is that purpose? How do we measure that purpose or identify what it is and whether people are living according to their true purpose? Science has no answers but it can't say that it can't answer. Thus for science to suggest life or the universe has "deeper meaning" is blasphemy and a "purpose of life" is never taught in scientific circles. But by not teaching the purpose of life they are implicitly asserting that your life has no purpose. They don't have to say it to teach it. Likewise the idea that there is no soul and death ends one's existence/consciousness may not be explicitly stated but it's implied. Science believes the brain is our consciousness thus if the brain dies so must the conscious experiences. The trouble is they don't account for the heart or soul in consciousness since for life to exist when the physical body dies there must be some other substance that survives the body but thus far the soul has not been identified with scientific instruments. Hence to empiricists it doesn't exist since they can't measure it. That too is why empiricism is so idiotic since existence to them changes according to their technology. Cave-men empiricists would say stuff like radio and internet are crazy/impossible. Empiricists are the type where if someone time-traveled to our time from the future, in theory, they'd never believe it no matter what unless they personally went to the future themselves and personally traveled with the time-traveler from their time to our time. Even if the time-traveler went back in time with the present day empiricist they still wouldn't believe they were from the future unless they personally went to the future with them and back. Sadly Empirical thought poisons some sciences as well as philosophy, from which empiricism originates. However if we take the assumption of empirical science(philosophy) that the afterlife doesn't exist and life ends at death then what is the point of it all? Why care about stuff? Why do stuff? Why bother living life when it all ends at death eventually and there is no point to any of it?

Why suffer when it can just end via suicide? Because of people's feelings? Who cares when feelings are illusions and illogical biological constructs meant to encourage cooperation for survival? If we are just evolved animals and nothing really means anything special, except in our own imaginations and feelings why go through with it all? It is an undisputable fact that the hardships of life are greater than the pleasures of life, so if there is no afterlife suicide is the smart logical move for whoever suffers hardship, which is everyone. Honestly if there is no afterlife people should kill themselves because we are the worst type of species to populate this planet, the universe would be better off without humanity if there were no afterlife where the evil individual humans are justly punished for their crimes in full. Science again has no scientifically valid reason for humans to not just commit mass suicide to avoid hardship, scientifically science teaches that the self-suicide of our species would be a good thing. The problem is that most scientists have something in their heart that tells them that sound "scientific theory" just can't be right. Yet if life is meaningless without purpose then extinction would be smart from a scientific view and to live would be near criminal for humans to do, particularly when humans harm so many other life-forms even in the process of helping them. But then again why do we care about other life-forms and planets? Why not just blow up the whole universe? Really scientifically why shouldn't humans just blow the whole damn thing up ending all the suffering of everything in the Universe? Wouldn't that be heroic, if humans just destroyed the universe and thereby ended all worldly suffering for everything forever? Science has no answer for this. Then people wonder why suicide and immorality is on the rise. It really is because of the mainstream cult of science. Much of the technology science produces is good, although some is bad like atomic bombs, but theologically its filthy and misanthropic. Scientifically advanced robots would be the ultimate replacement for the human species. Some fear being replaced by advanced robots but scientifically this is the correct destiny of our species. Science teaches that ultimately it would be better if robots were the dominant life-form and humans were subservient to them or extinct. Science leads to no other outcome, unless religious apocalypse or human "devolution" interrupts/prevents the scientific replacement plan. Unfortunately this filthy scientific doctrine of pointless life leading to eventual self-extinction or extinction by robots (or aliens) is what is indirectly subliminally unintentionally taught in most science classes/lessons throughout the world. Secularist science teaches there is no standard of good/bad and that it's merely cultural superstition of whether something or someone is good or bad. It teaches us our "feelings" are just chemical reactions. The very notion of justice does not exist in the realm of scientific thought. Really there is no scientific reason to justify revenge or retaliation or punishment for people believing/saying/doing "evil" things. Because scientifically there is no way to label something evil. In reality we know some things are evil and deserve to be punished or avoided but science says that's just superstition and culture. That's why scientific atheists really do have no moral moral standard. It doesn't mean they are immoral or amoral people but science teaches morality is a human invention/illusion. And that's what true science as well as fake science teaches, so that's why true science is still semi-dangerous if taken as a faith. Science is a tool and it's one Satan can use against us. Recklessly though science and empiricism teach Satan doesn't even exist, so science truly has zero defense against Satan. A absolutist scientist is spiritually ignorant and defenseless. Science is only a human construction, it is a man-made methodology that sometimes functions as a religion or philosophy. Yet man-made constructions, like science, can be criticized and rejected; in totality or partially. Being scientific in itself simply means being scientific. It doesn't mean it's good/bad or right/wrong or civilized/sacreligious. Scientific approaches are not inherently better or correct, it's just a particular approach, unfortunately at sometimes given too little importance in history and sometimes given too much importance in history. To think everything that is scientific is good and everything unscientific is bad/wrong or invalid is to make science a religion and everything outside of science blasphemous heresy. Such an attitude towards science as the ultimate standard is to make science a religion or even God, with scientists as prophets. Afterall why else do you think scientists label their theories "laws" just as prophet's taught us "God's laws"? Remember science cannot establish laws as only God is the law-giver and every scientific law has loopholes that make the law invalid or inapplicable, especially when God is accounted for as God frequently breaks the "laws" of science without consequences. The problem with science today is many teach it as a religion without knowing by use of their vocabulary and resort to science as the ultimate standard of knowledge/judgement. If anyone ever mentions a scientific "law" then that is a religious statement and they have an unhealthy understanding/belief in science to be using such legislative terminology. At the minimum to "be scientific" is to have a prejudiced view that is intolerant of other viewpoints and methodologies and the conclusions derived from other viewpoints/methodologies/religions. While prophets were sometimes scientific, no prophet of God specified being scientific as a path to eternal success. Sadly the approach of the majority of people towards science throughout time has not been the same approach taught by the prophets. Science has benefitted mankind in many ways, but spiritually many people go astray regarding their relationship with science by treating/viewing/using it different than the ways the prophets of God did. The point is that Science, of all types in all time periods, does not lead to paradise.

You will never know everything, but you can learn what is false and most can also learn what is true, yet everyone is able to recognize falsehood if they are sincere and take time to acquire knowledge. Whether an individual learns or is able to learn the truth is irrelevant in some regards because nearly everyone, with few exceptions in the case of the mentally ill and such, can learn and identify most types of falsehood even if they never ever learn what is true. You don't need to know what the truth is in order to know what falsehood is. As any test-taker knows there are choices on the test which they know are false even if they aren't sure which available answer is true. The same applies to the test of life. When falsehood is revealed if a person knowingly follows it, then that person has rejected and denied the truth by not even trying to find it. If one chooses to accept a lie when they know it to be a lie, then they would not accept the truth even if they found the truth. To pick or stick to C when you know C is wrong, just because you don't know if A or B is right, is complete lunacy and unjustifiable. Sadly though with religions many will keep on believing or living like they are a member of a religion even after they know it's a false faith, simply for worldly reasons. That's unacceptable to God. You don't get points for picking/living the wrong answer, just because you knew it was wrong but picked/stuck to it for worldly reasons. If you know a religion is wrong then God wants you to act accordingly and that is the right religion. Internally people are hardwired by God to know this is true, unfortunately cowardice makes them choose not to want to know something is wrong so that they don't have to treat it as wrong and they think they are still a good person due to their ignorance of what is wrong and failure to reject the wrong. There is a distinct difference between not being able to know something and not wanting to know, many don't want to know because with knowledge comes accountability. There is a popular saying, "*Ignorance is bliss*", the Arabic name for Satan is Iblees and I suspect this saying also originates from him; because it certainly wasn't taught to us by the prophets. What you don't know can and will hurt you. Rather we should say, "*Ignorance is Iblees*". For example the people of Noah pbuh would put their fingers in their ears in order to avoid hearing what he had to say, because they didn't want to know. They wanted to keep living as they were even if it was sinful, they didn't want to hear Noah pbuh tell them they were wrong. Then on their deathbeds they would tell their kids to do the same thing they did to Noah pbuh instructing them to never abandon their forefathers idols making them promise to ignore and reject Noah pbuh. Thus the true religion of the people of Noah pbuh was not just idolatry but idolatry was simply a byproduct of family pride/arrogance. This false religion even exists today and I've witnessed my own relatives tell me in front of other relatives how they know everything and are always right because they are the oldest in the family. It wasn't even said as a joke either, it was kind of half-jokingly but most of the relatives present had no issue with the statement and thought it was just words or wisdom or that certain age where family members can no longer be refuted and chastised for being wrong. Age has nothing to do with whether someone is right or wrong, it's something to consider when correcting someone but one can never use someone's age as an type of immunity or intellectual and religious infallibility. Being old just means your old, that's it. Being old doesn't mean you're smart and likewise being young doesn't mean you're dumb. Seniority has nothing to do with authenticity and legitimacy of one's opinions or beliefs. Right is right and wrong is wrong, age has nothing to do with either. Likewise relative status doesn't mean anything. People say "Uncle so and so said...." or "Great Grandma so and so said......" or "My Mom/Dad told me...." and they think I'm supposed to respect that as if being an Uncle or Grandparent or Parent is an intellectual credential. Being a Mom/Dad just means they had sex and a kid was born, it doesn't mean they know anything at all even regarding sex. Likewise being a grandparent just means they had kids who had kids, it' doesn't mean what they believe/say/do is right because they are "Grandpa so and so". The same applies to "Uncles" and "Aunts", that's the worst one in my opinion because to be an uncle or aunt all you gotta do is be alive and have a brother or sister that has kids, that's literally all it is. The title "uncle" or "aunt" just means "one of my siblings has kids". Yet so many tribalistic people think these titles of familial relationships add weight/wisdom to one's words, actions or beliefs. Do you know how common it is to have a kid and be a parent? Or a grandparent? Or an Uncle/Aunt? Or Brother/Sister? Everybody's got parents except Adam and Eve, and everybody's got grandparents and many have uncles/aunts and brothers and sisters and kids as well. Your Parent/Grandparent/Sibling/Relations don't deserve extra credit in the intellectual or religious sphere of knowledge, opinions, sayings or actions. Whether it's an opinion, belief, saying or deed of a relative or a stranger makes absolutely no difference. In fact sometimes it's best to give extra credibility to a stranger to compensate for the family prejudice and bias naturally given to kinship. You cannot give extra points to relatives thinking they are more likely to be right, wise or good just because they are related to you. To do so is unjust. Relatives are wrong just as often as the people you aren't related to. Every family is full of idiots including your own, so don't ever think that because they are your family then that means their opinions, beliefs, sayings, actions aren't utterly stupid or satanic. Your family is not immune from extreme ignorance and incompetence regarding religion and how to go to paradise. You might like them to be immune to idiocy, evil, hell and the wrath of God but God won't treat them any differently than anyone else just because they're "your family" and you "care so much about them". God loves/hates people according to his own criteria, your feelings towards family and other people are not factors in God's attitude toward them or their status/intelligence. Don't expect your family or friends to know or teach you the authentic important information about religion that you need to know, believe or act upon. The majority of people don't know, believe or act accordingly and die ignorant and go to hell even though their families and friends tell each other differently. No matter what people say or think, God says who goes to paradise and who goes to hell. God doesn't treat people based on how they believe they'll be treated when they die or how others think they'll be treated, he treats us exactly the way how he told the prophets to tell us how he treats people when they die. If you are ignorant of the afterlife and the detailed prophetic information of what will happen after death, then you are like the person trying to travel without knowing the directions and are unlikely to reach the destination you intend. Some people may say that it's impossible to know what happens after death because nobody has come back from the dead to tell, but this is another cop out and way of avoiding the truth. We would never say that it's impossible to know what happened in the past because nobody from the past has ever time-traveled and told us, because you don't need to hear it firsthand from someone who's been through it to know it. Likewise some types may say, "*I told so and so to give me a message when they died if there was a heaven or hell and which religion is true and they never gave me a message. So it must be a myth and death is a state of non-existance.*" There are many fun ways to refute this. One could ask "*Well did you bury them with a cellphone so they could call you? And do you know if the phone has reception, power, minutes and service? Did you bury them with a laptop so they could send you an email? And does it have internet service, and do they remember their email password or your email address? Or maybe they wrote a letter with the writing utensils you buried them with and the postal service has just lost it in the mail? Maybe they lost the stamps or couldn't afford to send it? Have you asked the post office if this dead person has sent you any letters from the mailbox at their grave? Maybe they tried to stop by but your appearance changed since they saw you last and they didn't recognize you so they gave the message to someone else instead? Could it be that maybe they just forgot about you or lied when they made such a promise to you? Maybe they have a big list of things to do now that they're dead and they just haven't gotten around to you yet?*" When they say no to any of these questions then you can ask "*Well then how are they supposed to send you a message? Clearly they don't have the means to send you a message from the grave so that's why you haven't gotten any messages.*"

81

If someone says to let them know when I go to the toilet and I don't, that doesn't mean I never went to the toilet, that just means I didn't tell you either because I couldn't or I didn't want to. If someone can expect the dead to clue them in on the afterlife then I can expect a living person to tell me when they are dreaming. Now I have absolutely no strictly secular scientific evidence to suggest people have a vivid life-like experience while they sleep, known as a dream. One can say, "*I think everyone is just making it all up and nobody has ever had a dream it's all a lie. If you say I've had a dream so I should know then I want you to scientifically prove I've had a dream and tell me what it was. Where is your proof that I've ever had a dream?*" Now one could scientifically say, "*The only way people can prove to me that dreams are real is if they tell me while they are asleep in their dream exactly what is going on to them in their dream. I don't want to hear some story after they wake up. While they are asleep I want them to somehow give me a sign or message to let me know that they are currently dreaming AND I want to know exactly what's happening to them in their dream while they are experiencing it. No matter where I am on the planet and where they are they must send me this message while they are asleep and I am awake and it must tell me all that I want to know. If they can't then dreams aren't real. Also they must prove what they say their dream was about as well, so I know they aren't making it all up.*" Such a request is only reasonable, right? No it's completely stupid! Those who are sleeping cannot send messages to those who are awake, even if before they go to sleep they get told to send a message if they have a dream and they sincerely promise to send a message when/if they have a dream. Likewise the dead cannot send a message to the living. Just because they don't send messages doesn't mean nothing is going on, that just means they aren't communicating with you. People who are alive and in prison can't even communicate with the living because they aren't allowed to, so what do you expect the dead to do? We don't need an interview with the deceased to be aware of what happens in the afterlife because God has sent revelation to us through his prophets to tell us. Such a person who requires an interview with the dead before they believe are the same types of people who rejected the prophets in their own lifetime for the same exact reasons. Previous prophets were explicitly rejected by people who witnessed their miracles firsthand because they refused to believe what the prophets said about the afterlife, citing that they never met anyone who came back from the dead to tell them so they thought the prophets were making stuff up. These are the type who will worship the antichrist because he will have 2 jinn pose as a person's dead parents and the jinn will tell them to worship the antichrist and they will obey thinking it was their dead parents. The problem with such people is arrogance, because they are too arrogant to admit that God would give knowledge that they don't have to someone else whom they consider inferior to themselves. Because of their arrogance they choose to remain in ignorance. If a person chooses to remain ignorant of God and would rather live their life without religion, or without researching to find the true religion, then they are in essence choosing this life over the afterlife and their desires over the Creator. This is why people will be given eternal bliss or eternal punishment despite only having lived one life for a short amount of time. Some may say that's not fair and that people should only be punished for as many years as they lived and did bad. However in that short lifetime people prove who they really are. If someone lives their whole life witnessing all kinds of signs from God over and over again guiding them towards the truth and then still after all that they die rejecting the truth it wouldn't matter if they lived for eternity, they'd still reject the truth. That's why such people are punished in hell for eternity without relief. The length of time during which a crime was committed has nothing to do with the duration of punishment one is sentenced to. This is why doing a crime for 5 minutes doesn't equal 5 minutes of jail time. Conversely nobody ever complains that believers get to be in paradise forever despite only living a short time.

It is impossible for someone to believe in God and when God sends a book or a prophet they refuse to follow the latest prophet and his message. If you claim to believe in God and God sends a book, then you are expected to accept and follow it. It's irrational for one to say, *"Well I believe in God, so I don't need to read his latest book"*. God doesn't waste our time sending books or prophets we don't need. God created the time we have and has the right to tell us what to do with it. Who do you think you are to say that you are too busy to read the book God sent? What possible excuse could you have when God gave you eyes, ears, a mind, hands and all the faculties necessary to learn what his book says? You cannot just follow the oldest book and think that will be acceptable, you live in this time so you need to follow the prophet of your time and the book of your time. If you are not following the latest edition of revelation, then you are following an outdated religion. Just try only obeying the original laws of your country, ignoring all the laws that came into effect after the constitution was written and see what happens when you use the excuse: *"I'm following the laws as they were when the country was founded in the beginning and don't have time to keep up to date with the new laws"*. Such an excuse would be seen as foolish and punishable which is why they say "Ignorance of the law is no excuse". Fortunately Allah will give people an excuse if they have legitimate reasons for not knowing what is sinful and what isn't, but that is different than the one who purposely remains ignorant because they are afraid to know. What if someone never had an opportunity to learn the true religion, or only heard a distorted version of the message the prophet of their time came with? What if they lived in a time between the prophets where the truth was not accessible to them? What if they were blind, deaf and dumb never learning one thing about any religion and lived their whole life in a vegetative state? Such a person would still have a natural disposition to worship the Creator because it is hardwired into us. No matter what a person's religious instruction may have been, when they are in serious life threatening danger they always know God is the only one who can save them and say, "*O God Help me!*" Unless they have been severely brainwashed at baptism, no one asks for Jesus pbuh or Buddha to save them because when our life is on the line we know that only the Creator has the power. Likewise even when cursing things people use the name of God instead of Jesus or others. But what if this person forgot and genuinely never had a chance to follow the true religion, what would happen to them? God is not unjust and will never punish someone in hell unless they deserve it, however keep in mind it is according to whether God thinks such a person deserves it, not according to their own arrogant feelings of specialness and privilege. No one will be in hell thinking that a mistake was made and that they were supposed to be in paradise, all the inhabitants of the hellfire will know exactly why they are there. On the Day of Judgment a person with a valid excuse who had no way to learn about the truth will be given a special test, the test will reveal whether they would have believed or disbelieved had the message of the true religion came to them. Their test will be that they will be given a special messenger from God and told to enter the real hellfire, those who obey will be saved and go to paradise, those who refuse to obey will end up in hellfire forever. We have the opportunity to enjoy the life of a believer and paradise if we accept the truth. We don't have an excuse. It's simple to get to paradise, all that is required is for you to believe and obey with sincerity. The key is to believe the truth about God and worship the Creator correctly not having any wrong ideas about him. Secondly to believe in all the messengers God has sent before your time that you know of and most importantly the prophet of your time, so that you can follow the legal code of your time. Sincerity is what separates believers from the hypocrites, as well as those that believe and obey only because it's convenient, or for reasons other than for the sake of God. There is 1 God, 1 human species, all the prophets taught 1 religion, so there can only be 1 way to get to paradise. Since there are only 2 possible destinations, heaven or hell, then that means there are really only 2 types of religions. There is the 1 true religion which leads to paradise, and then there are all the false religions which lead to hell. The question is not whether all religions lead to heaven, because all except 1 will lead to hell. That only 1 religion can be true is already established. Likewise it has already been established that you can discover which religion is true before your death. Thus there are really only 2 important questions to ask, both of which all will soon know the answers to.

1. *"Which is the 1 true religion?"*

and

2. *"Will you believe in it, accept it and die practicing it?"*

Many people are befuddled with the reason why everyone doesn't believe in the same religion if they were all made by the same God if God wants everyone to believe the same thing and follow the same religion. Those who are religiously astute will note that one reason why people don't all agree upon the same true religion is because of freewill. Which when combined with Satan, human desires and stupidity/arrogance can explain why some people don't believe in the true religion. They will answer that God allows disbelief because if God forced everyone to believe in the truth then it wouldn't be voluntary or sincere. This is true but it doesn't satisfy the skeptic disbeliever who thinks that the existence of a different opinion means there is no absolute truth of which all the other opinions are inferior and hateworthy in comparison to. They are the types who struggle to accept the idea that only 1 religion can be true because they believe in the religion of equality and that everyone is equally cared about by God because all of us were created by God. Yet that notion is false because God created other things too, but none would say God cares as much about trees, water, worms, rocks, birds, and fish equally as he cares about humans. So all creatures have individual relationships with God that determines how God views and feels towards them. Sometimes God can love animals more than humans as in the case of Noah pbuh or God can care more about humans than animals by the fact that we can eat animals while few animals eat us. The same applies to us eating plants with few plants eating us as a sign of God caring more for some creatures than others in some respects. Yet eating in itself doesn't prove God's love or care as being greater because if it did then microbes would be the most loved creatures since they eat us and most dead things. Also since worms eat humans, then based on the doctrine of "food chain love" we'd assume God loved worms more than us, but the food chain doesn't indicate who or what God cares most about. Of course some may claim that worms only eat humans after they are dead, but the same can be said of most animals which humans eat. While worms do indeed eat live humans too, as in the case of intestinal worms and many other types that can eat one's brain or cause blindness. So being the top of the food chain doesn't mean that God values you more than the food you eat. God could love what one eats more than he does the one doing the eating. Afterall what sin have the plants and animals who get eaten ever done? In comparison what sins have the ones eating the plants and animals done? Although this doesn't mean plants and animals are by default better than sinners, because God loves and forgives those sinners who repent sincerely in the prophetic manner. So being a sinner doesn't mean God cares more about what you are eating for dinner than he does you, but it could depending on the sinner and the circumstances. Thus all humans who eat things are not equal, some eaters are valued less by God than the food which they eat. Afterall no animals or plants will burn in hell, yet in this world they will get eaten by people who will dwell in hell forever. However despite this reality humans have rights that allow them a priority over animals and plants in many aspects, contrary to what misanthropists satanically suppose. Yet the disbeliever who doesn't believe in the notion of disbelievers, unless they count atheists, may then think that God loves all humans equally since we are the same species. This is disproven by the example of Noah's people and the natural feelings we ourselves have for other humans in that we don't all think of or love each other the same when we are the same species. This is because our dispositions towards people tend to be based on what those people believe, say and do, then in response to their beliefs, statements and actions we rate them accordingly in comparison with everyone else we know of. Even amongst ourselves there are no 2 people whom we care about with exactly identical amounts of love or hate whatever the case may be. There is someone you love more than all the rest and someone you hate more than all the rest, even though both are humans. Thus God is no different and does not love all equally nor hate all equally because humans are not equal. The idea of human equality is simply a false religion. As is human superiority, lets not forget there are the species of creatures called Jinn and the species called Angels. The religious belief of human equality leads those who believe in it to disbelieve in the very idea of there being such a thing as a false religion, since they want God to care about everyone equally; mainly because they hate the idea that God could care about someone else more than them. Particularly someone alive today, especially someone they think is inferior to themselves. They don't like the fact that God has favoritism based on every individual's faith and piety. So to avoid saying *"God doesn't like anyone on earth more than me."* they just say God loves everybody equally. But what they really mean and believe and feel is that nobody else is closer to God than they are because they think they are the greatest person on earth today. Yet the idea of human equality as regards what God thinks and feels about humans is too easy of an idea to refute since it is illogical. Plus we must remember the main reason they have this attitude is because they don't want to change their religion and abandon the false faith they are upon. So their end goal is to be left alone upon whatever wrong religion they are upon living the sinful life they are living and to have you shutup and stop making them feel wrong or bad due to their religion or sinful lifestyle. Basically they feel insecure that God might not like them or hate them for who they are. However insecurity about your relationship with God is necessary to have the correct healthy relationship with God as befits him as God and you as his creation. If you don't feel your relationship with God is vulnerable and there is a chance of rejection due to your beliefs or actions then you can never truly feel love from God. Since to feel true love there must be the possibility of there being no love. This is the problem with Christianity and Judaism, they have no sense of vulnerability with their relationship with God. Jews think God loves them due to their race and Christians think God loves them so much automatically that he died for them or sent a son of his to die for them. Thus both the Jews and Christians are spiritually immature and have a "Baby Love" selfish attitude with God where they expect God to love them and only wonder about how much God loves them rather than if. Truly Judaism and Christianity fundamentally teach that God loves you and/or everyone by default and it's only a question of how much do you want God to love you, thus they do good and avoid evil only to get more love never to avoid/decrease God's hatred. It is because of this doctrine of special unconditional love as taught by Judaism and Christianity combining with the doctrines of freedom of belief and human equality along with arrogance and Satanic influences that cause people to think that God doesn't love only the people of 1 religion while hating all the rest and that if God did then everyone would agree. This belief is also similar to what ancient pagans believed about religion. Today people took this notion and mixed it with freedom and equality, so they think God has to distribute his love for people equally and that exercising freedom cannot cause God to stop loving or start hating them. This is because the American drafters of the "Declaration of Independence" taught: *"God created mankind equal and all have the God-given right to life, liberty and the pursuit of happiness (freedom)"* and people believe what these prophets of Americanism said about God making everyone equal and giving them these rights such as "*the right to do what makes you happy and believe what you want*". Therefore when confronted with the prophetic doctrine that God only loves believers and hates all disbelievers they postulate an emergency Satanic response saying "*If God wanted everyone to believe the same thing then why don't we?*" To which the standard refutation is because of freewill, which means people can choose to disbelieve and be wrong because they are stupid and influenced by Satan or prefer falsehood and evil to truth and good. However they tend not to like this response and they have a good reason to reject the freewill refutation. Because even though God can't force people to believe, he could help everyone to all agree if he wanted to. They are correct on that point and freewill alone cannot refute that point. So this doctrine of multiple religions meaning God must like them all is totally nonsense, that exists because people feel entitled to be loved by God just because they were created. Arrogance of humans leads them to think we are equal and that God should treat us all equal as well. However the mere existence of different opinions does not mean a single one of those opinions has any validity whatsoever, especially when it comes to religion. Nor does a difference of opinion mean all are invalid either, which is the 2nd emergency excuse in that they'll say "*Either all of the religions are right and acceptable to God or everybody on earth is wrong.*" Yet to think that is to be an intellectual absolutist of the extremist variety, which again is due to a "pro-equality complex" where either everyone is right or everyone is wrong because they can't comprehend that people are not equal to each other or that God has favoritistic traits. It's very simple to understand that only 1 religion is correct, that's what every prophet taught. So then why doesn't God help people so that everyone chooses to believe in and practice the correct religion? Afterall Satan is our enemy so what chance do we have if God doesn't guide everybody? Is it not unfair for God not to guide everyone if God also created Satan too? First of all

God does help everyone to see Islam is true and all the other faiths are false, but some don't recognize the help and/or ignore the signs they get. They think if religious diversity is confusing to them and the majority are all on different religions, then God must not have a special policy towards 1 faith and it's adherents over others, or else he'd help everyone to join the right religion. Essentially they have a democratic attitude in that only a majority opinion can declare something to be right. They think this because they think God loves everyone or at least the majority, but they do have a point even though their notion of God loving all or all equally or the majority is false. The correct question people who doubt 1 faith having a "monopoly on salvation" should ask is, "*Why doesn't God help everyone believe in and practice the right religion?*" That is the correct question to ask. If they want to really know they have to ask the right question first if they really want to learn answers. Most don't ask this question though because they don't really want an answer but are asking sarcastically thinking they already know and have the answer. The freewill refutation doesn't work if they ask the correct question because its a question of God giving direct guidance so it becomes extremely easy for all to believe, to the point that all do believe because God makes everyone know how evil and wrong all the false religions are and how true and right the one correct religion is. Afterall doesn't God want everyone to believe in the true religion? Well the answer is simply no. God doesn't want everyone to believe in the correct religion because if he truly did then we all would. So you really do have to be honest and admit that, "*Yes God could guide everybody to believe in the 1 true religion, but God just doesn't want to.*" That's right, it's true, God does not want every human to be sinless and worship him. Do you know why? Because God already has creatures who do 100% what God wants them to do. They are called angels. Every angel believes in the right thing, does the right thing and never sins. So those who insist God could make everyone believe and stop us from doing evil if he wanted to are right, God could, but he doesn't

91

want to because he already has angels to be like that so why create a repeat species of angels? Is there some rule that says God can only create angels and no other type of creature? Why do humans think God can only create angels or it's unfair? God is creative and doesn't want to only create angels, God wants plants, animals, humans, devils, etc because it displays his immense power and to truly understand why you would need the knowledge of God anyways. Yet lets consider some attributes of God such as being forgiving and merciful. Now if nobody ever disobeyed God then how could God be forgiving if he never forgave anybody for doing wrong? God could not be forgiving if nobody ever sinned so God could forgive them. God is also the most severe in punishment, but if God never punished anybody how could he be the most severe in punishment? Basically for God to be God as God has defined himself then God has to act accordingly and since God is merciful there must be opportunities to display that mercy, so by us humans existing and repenting it allows God to be merciful and forgive, likewise humans existing and not repenting from disbelief or sins shows God as forbearing and then as just when God finally does punish the guilty ones. So the existence of human freewill shows the depth and complexity of God, because if only angels existed that would be a very bland boring one dimensional under-developed God. Such a "god" would have an ungodly personality/character that would be emotionally inferior to us. For such a "god" to exist would be impossible because by definition the Creator must be more complex than its creation, so God could never give us such a wide range of attributes or characteristics if God was such a undeveloped entity that was less complex than its creatures. Emotionally God must be more complex than us, but God couldn't be if everyone believed and obeyed. If God created only angels or 100% obedient beings and nothing else then that would be an uncreative and nearly insecure God rather than the full God we have which can create such a diverse universe and have such a wide range of various treatments for the things within it. God allows falsehood to exist so God can prove he and his truth destroys all falsehood, God could say it but to prove it is a different matter. God proves all that he lets us know about himself, God isn't "just talk". Similarly since God is the one who guides, some creatures need to be misguided in order for God to guide them. Also if all were guided by God then that guidance wouldn't be anything special since it would be generic and guidance would practically be expected as if we "deserve to be guided". Whereas that's basically the issue with the confused people who can't understand religious diversity failing to undermine the fact that one religion has exclusivity of the truth. These types of people expect that all humans "deserve" to know what is true and false, right and wrong, before they die. They think we "*deserve to go to paradise, just because we are human*" and that "*nobody can ever deserve to go to hell because we are human and can never be that bad*". If you ask them point-blank this is what they believe, that everyone deserves to go to paradise and they think it's unfair for God to not guide those he chooses not to guide. Or they try to blame their badness on God and say it's God's fault they are bad so therefore it's unfair for them to be punished because of their decisions. Basically they think freewill is unfair, but many also think "freedom" is a "right", so they actually just believe that it's unfair for God to give them freewill and expect responsibility. They think God shouldn't let them be evil if he doesn't want them to be evil, but that's like a child telling a parent that they shouldn't ever allow any possibility for them to break any rules if they really don't want them to break the rules. Such an argument is crazy because only an irresponsible person would make such a claim. Responsibility is a fact of life, just because people don't like the consequences of their beliefs/actions doesn't mean there is anything wrong with responsibility. Without responsibility one cannot succeed or get rewarded. If there is no possibility of failure no success or reward can ever exist. Hence for Heaven to exist as a possibility then Hell must exist or else that would not be just. It's not like God doesn't help us at all, that would be unfair. God actively tries to guide everybody as much as he can without making the test of life invalid. For you to get the reward for passing the test of life, God can't take it for you or make it impossible for you to fail because then it wouldn't be a true test and there would be no justifiable reason/excuse to give you any rewards at all. God chooses to guide or allows people to go astray based on them and whether they truly want guidance to submit or not. All have an equal opportunity, but God gives extra help only to those who truly want it and appreciate it. God won't go out of the way to guide people who don't sincerely want God's help on the test of life. On a personal and general level God wants every individual to believe correctly but legally God doesn't want 100% believers. Since if everyone passed the test of life then that would be an unfair test that in effect means it's impossible to fail since nobody failed it. Another reason for the existence of false religions is because if 100% of people believed then lots of the benefits of disbelief and disbelievers would not exist. Yes, false religions and disbelievers actually do have a positive effect on the world and God desires this positive effect of disbelief and disbelievers even though God hates disbelief and disbelievers. An example is Satan. God hates Satan but he allows him to exist despite that hatred because he is more pleased with the long-term effects that Satan's actions bring about than God would be if Satan didn't exist at all. The benefit of Satan existing is greater than his harm, the same applies to false religions. Yet some think if they use some religious terms then their doctrine about multiple religions being valid will somehow count. Thus I've met people who say "If God wanted everyone to believe in just 1 particular religion then why were there 12 tribes of Israel?" This type of question infuriates me. 1. Israel is the name of the prophet Jacob who had 12 kids, including the prophet Joseph pbuh. They all had the same religious beliefs. They were just called the 12 tribes because those 12 kids of Jacob had lots of descendants to the point that 12 large tribes came about, with each tribe being the progeny

94

of 1 of Jacob's 12 sons. This is why sometimes the members of those 12 tribes are called the "Children of Israel" or the "Nation of Israel". To say that God allows for multiple religions and doesn't want everyone to believe in just 1 religion because there are 12 tribes of Israel instead of 1 is equivalent to saying that "*If God wanted everyone to believe the same religion then in the beginning why did he make 2 people, 1 man and 1 woman? If only 1 religion is true then why were there two genders of people and not 1? And why did Adam and Eve have more than one child if there is only 1 true religion? If there is only 1 way the 1 God wants us to worship him then why does more than 1 person exist?*" Whereas anyone who understands religion will realize how stupid and invalid such questions are. Such questions are so foolish they are dangerous and that's how you know such questions come from Satan and not the idiot themselves. Thus don't call them an idiot because they are really just parroting what Satan tells them to say so you get mad and stop trying to guide the person. Yet some people persist in giving me such responses when I invite them to become Muslims insisting they either join Islam or tell me why they think it's wrong so I can quit because only 1 religion counts and I want us both to go to paradise and can't stand the two of us not being on the same path to paradise. I offer such challenges to kafirs because truly they have no good reason to reject Islam and if/when they realize this then many of them try to attack the idea that only 1 religion is true so they can end the conversation without having to change their life or tell me to change mine, which they usually can't effectively try to do. The challenged who reply with something like the 12 tribes question is simply their emergency excuse for them to try to maintain the religious status quo and get back to "having fun with their life doing whatever they want to do". However the Quran mentions such people and such excuses in 2:122-141 which in english means,

"O Children of Israel! Remember My favour wherewith I favoured you and how I preferred you to (all) creatures. And guard (yourselves) against

a day when no soul will in aught avail another, nor will compensation be accepted from it, nor will intercession be of use to it; nor will they be helped. And (remember) when his Lord tried Abraham with (His) commands, and he fulfilled them, He said: Lo! I have appointed thee a leader for mankind. (Abraham) said: And of my offspring (will there be leaders)? He said: My covenant includeth not the disbelievers and wrong-doers. And when We made the House (at Mecca) a resort for mankind and sanctuary, (saying): Take as your place of worship the place where Abraham stood (to pray). And We imposed a duty upon Abraham and Ishmael, (saying): Purify My house for those who go around and those who meditate therein and those who bow down and prostrate themselves (in worship). And when Abraham prayed: My Lord! Make this city a place of security and bestow upon its people fruits, such of them as believe in Allah and the Last Day, He answered: As for him who disbelieveth, I shall leave him in contentment for a while, then I shall compel him to the doom of Fire - a hapless journey's end! And when Abraham and Ishmael were raising the foundations of the House, (Abraham prayed): Our Lord! Accept from us (this duty). Verily You, only You, art the All-Hearer, the All-Knower. Our Lord! And make us submissive unto Thee and of our offspring a nation submissive unto Thee, and show us our ways of worship, and relent toward us. Truly You are the one who accepts repentance the most merciful. Our Lord! And raise up in their midst a messenger from among them (the people of Mecca, of the offspring of Ishmael) who shall recite unto them Your Verses and instruct them in the Book (this Qur'ân) and Al-Hikmah (full knowledge of the Islâmic laws and jurisprudence or wisdom or Prophethood), and purify them. Verily! You are the All-Mighty, the All-Wise." And who turns away from the religion of Abraham (Islâm) except him who befools himself? Truly, We chose him in this world and verily, in the Hereafter he will be among the righteous. When his Lord said to him, "Submit (be a Muslim)!" He said, "I have submitted myself (as a Muslim) to the Lord of the 'Alamîn (mankind, jinn and all that exists)." And this (submission to Allâh, Islâm) was enjoined by Abraham upon his sons and by Jacob, (saying), "O my sons! Allâh has chosen for you the true religion, then die not except in the Faith of Islâm." Or were you witnesses when death approached Jacob?

When he said unto his sons, "What will you worship after me?" They said, "We shall worship your Ilâh (God - Allâh), the Ilâh (God) of your fathers, Abraham, Ishmael, Isaac, One Ilâh (God), and to Him we submit (in Islâm)." Those are a people who have passed away. They shall receive the reward of what they earned and you of what you earn. And you will not be asked of what they used to do. And they say, "Be Jews or Christians, then you will be guided." Say (to them), "Nay, (We follow) **only the religion of Ibrâhim (Abraham), Hanifa** *[Islâmic Monotheism, i.e. to worship none but Allâh (Alone)], and he was not of Al-Mushrikûn (those who worshipped others along with Allâh)." Say, "We believe in Allâh and that which has been sent down to us and that which has been sent down to Abraham, Ishmael, Isaac, Jacob, and to Al-Asbât [the offspring twelve sons of Jacob], and that which has been given to Mûsa (Moses) and Isâ (Jesus), and that which has been given to the Prophets from their Lord. We make no distinction between any of them, and to Him we have submitted (in Islâm)." So if they believe in the like of that which you believe, then they are rightly guided, but if they turn away, then they are only in opposition. So Allâh will suffice for you against them. And He is the All-Hearer, the All-Knower. [Our Sibghah (religion) is] the Sibghah (Religion) of Allâh (Islâm) and which Sibghah (religion) can be better than Allâh's? And we are His worshippers. Say* **"Dispute you with us about Allâh while He is our Lord and your Lord? And we are to be rewarded for our deeds and you for your deeds. And we are sincere to Him [in worship and obedience (we worship Him Alone and none else, and we obey His Orders).]" Or say you that Abraham, Ishmael, Isaac, Jacob and Al-Asbât [the offspring twelve sons of Jacob] were Jews or Christians? Say, "Do you know better or does Allâh (know better that they all were Muslims)? And who is more unjust than he who conceals the testimony he has from Allâh?** *And Allâh is not unaware of what you do." Those are a people who have passed away. They shall receive the reward of what they earned, and you of what you earn. And you will not be asked of what they used to do."*

The Arabic Quran is the direct message from the Creator which guides to the truth and paradise, which remains in the same form as revealed to God's prophet Muhammad pbuh in the first person. It is the final revelation that completes and perfects mankind's religion. I have researched every major religion practiced in the world today and many of the minor religions and found Islam to be the only true religion. But do not take my word for it, I simply ask you to do your own genuine research about Islam yourself, with an open mind. You have nothing to lose, absolutely nothing. If Islam is false then you will be able to tell and will be more confident in whatever religion you have right now, or at least one step closer to the truth whatever it is. If Islam is true then you will have the opportunity to obtain eternal bliss in the afterlife with inner peace and purpose in this life. At the minimum you would have a better understanding of nearly 2 billion people on the planet and be less likely to believe a lie when it is told to you. What if Muhammad pbuh really is the final messenger of our Creator? Would you follow him and the rest of the prophets to paradise? Or would you reject it even if it was proven without a doubt to be the truth to you? What if the Quran is a direct message from your Creator and after me informing you about this fact you scoff at it and never bother to look into it, how do you think your Creator will treat you on the Day of judgment if you die in that condition? On that day you won't be able to say you didn't have time, or that no one ever warned you. You have time now. Type "*Free Quran*" into any internet search engine and you can get a free Quran or a translation or the Arabic with a translation in electronic, audio or physical form. You were destined to read this, it is no random coincidence or accident. The important question is what will you do with the rest of your life? More research would be my suggestion. However at the very minimum you know now that religious equality is a myth. So never believe again that all people are equal. For that belief leads to eternal hell regardless of what faith is true.

www.ingramcontent.com/pod-product-compliance
Lightning Source LLC
Chambersburg PA
CBHW061706120626
46550CB00003B/1106